T0368346

In His Hands

In His Hands

Angela Mullins

WESTBOW
PRESS®
A DIVISION OF THOMAS NELSON
& ZONDERVAN

WestBow Press books may be ordered through booksellers or by contacting:

WestBow Press
A Division of Thomas Nelson & Zondervan
1663 Liberty Drive
Bloomington, IN 47403
www.westbowpress.com
1 (866) 928-1240

ISBN: 978-1-9736-7791-8 (sc)
ISBN: 978-1-9736-7792-5 (hc)
ISBN: 978-1-9736-7790-1 (e)

Library of Congress Control Number: 2019917138

Print information available on the last page.

WestBow Press rev. date: 6/3/2020

Acknowledgments

Writing a book was harder than I thought and more rewarding than I could have ever imagined. Turning my messy journaling into a book was as hard as it sounds. The experience was challenging and rewarding. There are numerous influential people in my life. This journey would not have been possible without the support of these special people.

I am thankful first and foremost for my heavenly Father. Without my faith in Him, I would not be the person I am today. I thank Him for giving me Bracey.

I wish to thank Torrey, my loving and supportive husband. We've journeyed the same life together. You have been my rock. You have helped me see the positives in every situation. You have cried with me and laughed with me. You have held me and listened to me. You continued to encourage me to finish my book even when I accidentally lost most of it and wanted to throw in the towel. You helped me remember the purpose of my writing. I love you and look forward to spending the rest of my life with you.

Thank you, Bracey, Brynn, and Brevin, for keeping me young. Your smiles and laughs are contagious. I love being your mom. It truly is the toughest but most gratifying job I'll ever have. I love you.

I am grateful to my parents, Kevin and Tina Nichols, who

supported us emotionally and financially. Thank you for opening your home up to us when we needed it most. We will never be able to repay you for the sacrifices you have made. Dad, thank you for the special bond you have made with Bracey. You truly are one of his absolute favorite people. You have been to every single surgery. You have faithfully been by our side through the tough times and the exciting times. Mom, thank you for being an ear for me. Thank you for always doing our laundry every time we visit. Thank you for always dropping everything to be there for me. Thank you both for continually loving and putting your children and grandchildren first. I love you.

Thank you to my siblings, Alisa and her husband, Brock Glaze, and Scott and his wife, Ayda Nichols. Alisa and Brock, you guys were with us the first time Bracey stopped breathing. I will never forget the way you comforted us and prayed for us. Thank you for constantly being there for us. Alisa, thank you for being in the delivery room with me. I know you didn't know what to say, but thank you for just being there and making sure I was okay. Thank you for spending the first few weeks of Bracey's life with me. Your presence was reassuring. You and Mom kept things entertaining for me. I cherish your friendship. Scott, thank you for being a sounding board when I just needed to talk. You always understand me. Ayda, thank you for loving on my kids. I love you all.

Thank you to my Mullins family. We are a large family spread throughout the Midwest, yet I know that I can reach out to any of you for support or advice. I love the closeness our family shares. Thank you to my in-laws, Tom and Cathy Mullins, for your love and support. You have been at many of the surgeries and hospital stays. Cathy, thank you for always cleaning my house when you visit. I know I'll always have a super clean stove after you leave.

Tom and Amanda Mullins, thank you for the times you've taken care of Brynn. Tom, you always have words of wisdom, and you have such a compassionate heart. You have been by our side during many hospital stays. Amanda, you gave me my first journal, which grew my love for writing. Thank you for your friendship. Tiphanie and Chris Volkers, thank you for always having an open home for us. Anytime we need a distraction or to just get away, we know you will always welcome us into your home. Thank you, Tiph, for the many times you have joined me at the hospital or traveled with Bracey and me to doctor appointments. You always keep things upbeat. Thank you, Chris, for loving on my kids or for picking on them when they need it. Tim and Katie Mullins, although geography keeps us apart more than we'd like, I know you guys are always praying for us. Thank you for the continued texts and calls. Thank you, Tim, for coming out to Bracey's back surgery. You were a wonderful distraction. Tenisha and Jason Branim, thank you for your close friendship and support. Thank you, Tenisha, for taking some time off work to be with me after Bracey's hand surgery. Thank you, Jason, for being my shopping buddy when I needed a distraction. Thank you both for taking Brynn for us during Bracey's back surgery. Knowing she was with you guys gave me such peace while I was away from her. I love you, Mullins, and I will forever be grateful for the outpouring of love you have all given us.

Thank you to all seventeen of my nieces and nephews for loving, helping, and accepting Bracey. He and I love you all!

A special thank you to our dearest friends Greg and Angela Wright. You guys have been with us from the very beginning. You have cried, laughed, rejoiced, and prayed with us. You have been our solid rock when we felt helpless. Your friendship is truly an unconditional, everlasting friendship. I love you guys!

To Bracey's pulmonologist, your love for Bracey from day one has developed into a special bond between the two of you. Thank you for your aggressive approach to Bracey's health. Thank you for being honest with me. You are one of the main reasons Bracey is alive today. Thank you for learning the way Bracey's body responds to treatments. Thank you for your patience and for never making me feel rushed at our doctor visits. Thank you for loving Bracey and caring for him as one of your own children. Thank you for all the times you visited us in the hospital even when you weren't on call. We are truly blessed to have you as one of our special doctors. I love you.

Thank you to Bracey's orthopedic surgeon. I can't even think about where Bracey would be right now without you. I knew God had directed us to you the minute you walked into our room. Your smile and love for your patients is contagious. Thank you for having great patience with Bracey. The way you explain things for him to understand amazes me. Thank you for loving him as your own son. I will be forever grateful that we were referred to you.

Thank you to Bracey's gastroenterologist. You have been a wonderful doctor. Your soft-spoken voice brings a calming atmosphere. Thank you for your honesty and for listening to my concerns. I am truly blessed to have you as one of our doctors.

Thank you to all of our doctors and nurses that we have had over the years. Thank you for calming a hysterical, tired mother. Thank you for explaining a diagnosis multiple times to me. Thank you for your patience and love for helping kids become the best they can be. Your work is truly inspiring.

To my friends and family scattered around the country, thank you for your thoughts, prayers, phone calls, texts, and emails throughout the years.

Thank you to my friend and cover designer, Becky Williams.

You took my jumbled ideas and created the perfect cover for *In His Hands.*

Thank you to my brother-in-law, Chris Volkers, for offering a final read through to catch additional grammar errors and add a few suggestions.

Writing a book about the story of your life is a surreal process. I am forever appreciative to Janene Hudson for your awesome editorial skills. You helped bring my stories to life. It is because of your long hours of editing and your encouragement that my journaling has turned into this wonderful book. You forced me to make my dreams become a reality. Janene, I will be indebted to you forever. Thank you.

And lastly, a very special thank you to my very special son, Bracey. Your enthusiasm for life, love for God, love for others, contagious smile, and humor have completely changed my world. You inspire me to be a better person. You make me see the good in everything. When you're hurting, you make sure I'm okay. You are such a strong boy. I cannot wait to see what your future holds. I love you, buddy!

February 5, 2008

I was at my regular OB checkup to see how my baby and I were doing. I was thirty-eight and a half weeks pregnant, and I was so ready to have my first baby lying in the comfort of my arms. My doctor looked at me and, with a smile on her face, told me to head over to the hospital because my water was leaking. I was so ecstatic. After five long years of wanting and trying to get pregnant, our time was finally here. Nothing and nobody could ruin this day for me. The nursery was perfect. I had everything a healthy baby boy could ever need. Our lives were about to change. Torrey, my husband, and I could not wait to bring our son home.

Later that evening, when still no baby had arrived, my doctor ordered an ultrasound to take a look at the baby. She wasn't quite sure if she was feeling the head or the buttocks. She assured me this was just routine. *No big deal,* I thought. I had five of them in the last nine months, and he was always head down. The technician came in, and I got to see my little guy inside me one more time before he made his big entrance into the world. Yep, head was down, and he was in perfect position. That was a relief. I looked at Torrey and jokingly said, "Look at him and how he is holding his arms. He looks like a little frog. So cute!"

And so the waiting game continued. Two hours went by, and no change. I was still leaking a bit, which they checked with a very long Q-tip to see if it was amniotic fluid. Two more hours went by. No change. Two more hours went by. No change.

It had been ten hours, and I was exhausted and starving. Torrey was sound asleep in a chair in my room. My parents, mother-in-law, and sister were all sound asleep in the waiting room. I was resting in the bed when suddenly a downpour gushed out of my body. I yelled for Torrey, scaring the poor guy half to death, telling him my water just totally burst. He went out to get a nurse, who sweetly said, "We'll be right there."

Then, five minutes later, she came walking in with one of those long Q-tips. I said, "Oh, I don't think we are going to need that." Torrey and the nurse were standing in a puddle of water! The nurse could not believe her eyes. She said in all her years, she had never seen that much water. The contractions started almost immediately. *Yes*, I thought, *let's get this show on the road, so I can hold my baby!*

Time crept by, and I was getting very anxious. Another thirteen hours passed after my water burst, and our baby boy was finally ready to meet his parents. After an hour of painful pushing, Bracey made his way into the world at 2:30 p.m. on February 6, 2008. Everything changed.

Seconds after Bracey's birth, the room felt melancholy. I always imagined the feeling of holding my newborn baby on my chest immediately after birth. I couldn't wait to be the first one he saw and the one to warm and calm him. I couldn't wait to nurse him and to show him off to all of our family and friends. I couldn't wait to do all those things. But my plan was not God's plan. His plans were quite different.

As soon as Bracey made his appearance into the world, he was whisked away. The nurses were working on him. I couldn't see Bracey. He hadn't made a sound. The nurses had him on a warmer bed behind me, and I had no clue what was going on. It was silent except for the nurses whispering. I didn't know what they were saying or what was happening behind me. A nurse ran out of the room and quickly returned with a pediatrician. I still hadn't heard or seen my baby. My sister, Alisa, was by my side, and I could see the worry in her eyes. Torrey kept stepping away and then returning. He would rub my head and tell me everything was going to be okay. I could not get up. Nor could I see Bracey. I was an emotional basket case. I kept asking what was going on, but nobody really answered me. No one knew *how* to answer me. They just assured me he was breathing, and it would be okay. I saw nurses wipe tears from their eyes. After the doctor came in, he and the nurses quickly took our baby out of the room. I told Torrey to go with them; he needed to find out what was going on.

My parents and sister came into my room. They were doing their best to console me, but I wanted to know where my baby and husband went. I obviously knew something was wrong. Why wouldn't someone give me answers?

I gave birth at a smaller hospital, where the maternity ward was just not prepared for traumatic births, but the nursing staff was great. They came in and checked on me. I could tell they had been crying. They would not tell me anything about Bracey; they mainly tried to comfort me, reassuring me everything would be okay. Then they left.

Torrey came back in after a few minutes, which seemed like an hour, and I knew he had been crying. My parents kissed me, and along with my sister, they returned to the waiting room. I could tell Torrey was terribly shaken, but he tried so hard to be strong for me. Once we were alone in the room, he told me about Bracey. He said it took a long time for Bracey to breathe, and he was somewhat stable at the moment. I could tell he was fighting back the tears as he tried to explain what was going on. How do you tell your wife, who has just given birth, that this precious baby she wanted for so long was going to have to fight for his life?

With glossy eyes, he told me Bracey was breathing but would have to be transferred right away. They had made arrangements to transport Bracey to a nearby hospital with a neonatal intensive care unit (NICU). At that point, nobody knew what was wrong with him except that he needed special medical attention—fast. Torrey started crying. I knew there was more he wasn't telling me. I held his hands and said, "Please just tell me. What is it?"

With tears streaming down his face, Torrey took his hands and curled his wrists around his arms. He said Bracey's hands were curled all around his arms, and Bracey did not have any thumbs. I just wept and wept. He said he would like to go with Bracey. I knew that meant leaving me, but that was where he needed to be.

Having not seen my baby yet, I asked Torrey if I could please see Bracey before they left. The transport team wheeled him into my room in an incubator. I could see his little face and no more. I could not even touch him. They left, along with Torrey and Cathy, my mother-in-law. Although a few other family members were with me, I had never felt more alone than I did at that moment.

I immediately began talking to God. "Why, God? Why would You allow us to have a baby after so many years of waiting just to take him away? Why would You allow someone so small and precious to endure something so agonizing? Why are You doing this, God. Why? Are You punishing me for my sins? If so, please let me take Bracey's place. Please make me endure the pain and agony, not my baby boy. What are You trying to show me? Have I not been faithful to You? Please let me see my son again. Please let me hold him and hear his cry, Lord. I will give You all I have, Lord, but please don't take my baby away."

Finally, at the second hospital, Torrey was given some answers. The doctors and nurses were able to find out through an ultrasound and x-ray that Bracey's trachea had a hole in it and was attached to his stomach. His esophagus was not fully attached to his stomach. He had a form of scoliosis and hemi-vertebrae. He was missing both his thumbs and both radius bones, and his hands were wrapped around his arms. They called his condition VACTERL association.

The doctors knew Bracey needed to be transferred to a children's hospital. So that same evening, the transport team took Bracey to a large children's hospital in Chicago.

Seventeen hours after Bracey was born, I was walking out of my hospital and headed to see my baby. I was in physical and emotional pain, but I had to be near my son. On arrival, Torrey and I were greeted by a lot of our family. They waited in the NICU waiting room while Torrey and I went into the NICU. Bracey's nurse took me by the hand and led me over to him. She asked, "Would you like to hold him?" I was crying, smiling, and shaking. I sat in a recliner, and she handed me my son. Time stopped. Nothing in the world mattered to me at that moment. We still had no clue what God had in store for us, but it didn't matter. I was holding my precious son.

Shortly after, a doctor came in to explain Bracey's condition. VACTERL association is a nonrandom association of birth defects. Each letter stands for a defect.

- V = vertebral anomalies
- A = anal atresia (no hole at the bottom end of the intestine)
- C = cardiac defect, most often a ventricular septal defect
- TE = tracheoesophageal fistula (communication between the esophagus and trachea) with esophageal atresia (part of the esophagus is missing)
- R = renal (kidney) abnormalities
- L = limb abnormalities, most often radial dysplasia (abnormal formation of the thumb or the radius bone in the forearm)

Bracey had V, T, E, and L. The doctor went on to tell us Bracey would need surgery first thing in the morning in order to survive. The doctors needed to repair his trachea and esophagus. They were not sure if they would be able to do both at the same time, but they would try their best. The doctors told us this would be considered a major surgery and labeled it a level nine out of ten. I could not believe I still had tears to shed, but they were coming. My five-pound baby, just hours old, needed major open-chest surgery to survive.

My conversation with God continued. "Lord, what are You doing? Why didn't You allow the radiologist to find any of Bracey's birth defects before he was born? We had five ultrasounds done. Why couldn't you have given us a heads-up? We could have prepared for this, Lord. We love You and know Your ways are best. We know You have had this planned from the beginning of time. I just don't understand. Why Bracey? I love You and trust You, Lord. Please watch over my precious son. Please help me to understand why."

February 8, 2008—Twenty-Four Hours Old

The next morning came, and it was time for Bracey to go into surgery. Torrey and I held him for as long as we could. We arrived at the big red line on the hospital floor, and the nurse said we could not go any farther. We asked for one more minute. With tears pouring out of our eyes, we both held him, kissed him, and prayed with our precious son one more time before he was wheeled out of our sight. (I do believe the nurse was crying as well.) With tears streaming down our faces, we went to the waiting room, where our dearest family and friends were waiting.

Hours passed, and finally the doctor came in and explained Bracey was doing great! He was able to repair everything. It was a really long stretch to connect the two ends of the esophagus together, but he did it! He also separated Bracey's trachea from his esophagus.

The waiting room was no longer silent. Everyone cheered and embraced one another. I hugged the doctor, and then Torrey and I hugged for the absolute longest we have ever hugged. I remember him starting to let go, and I whispered, "Don't let go yet."

We knew Bracey would have a very long road ahead of him, but he was alive! He is our precious son, and he is a fighter!

Within the hour, Torrey and I were allowed to see Bracey. Our NICU nurse informed us how Bracey would look. She told us he would look even more fragile now than before surgery. He would have a ventilator down his throat, which was breathing for him. Bracey would be in an induced coma for a few days so his tiny body would have time to heal. He would have a chest tube to help with the fluid buildup. He would have a central line near his chest, which was placed to give him medications, nutritional fluids, or blood if need be. Torrey took my hand, and we walked down the NICU to Bracey's little bed.

Bracey seemed lifeless. Tears of heartache and relief rolled down my cheeks. I held his hand and spoke softly to him. Our nurse explained all of the different machines that he was hooked up to. We quickly became obsessed with his monitors. Our family came in a couple at a time. It truly helped the time pass.

The first evening after Bracey's surgery was upon us. Torrey had arranged for us to stay at the Ronald McDonald House. It was just a couple blocks away. I did not want to leave Bracey's side. It took Torrey a long time to convince me I needed to go and get some rest. He assured me if I woke up in the middle of the night, he would go back up to the NICU with me.

We both kissed Bracey good night and left for the RMH. The house was beautiful. For just a few minutes, my mind wasn't on leaving Bracey. Torrey showed me around the home. It was very nice. There were a lot of amenities for families. Then Torrey took me up to our room.

Just as we got off of the elevator, my heart broke into pieces. I started sobbing. I felt so far away from Bracey. Torrey hugged me and reassured me everything would be okay. I felt like I had lost a piece of me. Bracey and I were one for nine months, and then, within seconds, he was no longer with me. I missed feeling his little jabs and kicks. I missed feeling his hiccups. I longed to hold him, but all I could do was sit next to him and hold his hand. It wasn't enough. How would I get through this? I had never felt such pain and broken heartedness in all my life. Torrey hugged me again in the hall of the Ronald McDonald House and said he would hold me until I was ready to go in the room. I gathered myself, and we walked into the room where my mom and sister were waiting for us. They had arranged their schedules so they could stay with us for a while. It was a relief walking into that room and knowing we weren't going to be alone.

February 12, 2008—Six Days Old

Time seemed to have stood still. We sat and watched our little boy as he was in an induced coma for four days after his intense, major surgery. I found myself sitting by his little bed and watching the numbers on his monitor go up and down. I became obsessed with those numbers. At that point, my faith in God and those numbers were all I had to assure me Bracey was still breathing and was still fighting. I hadn't yet heard him cry; I hadn't seen his eyes; and I hadn't had the chance to feel his little hands squeeze my fingers.

My son looked so peaceful. I sat by him and sang and talked to him. I told him about Jesus and how much Jesus loved us and was going to allow us to be a family. I told him little stories of how his daddy and I met. I told him all about his grandparents, aunts, uncles, and cousins. I told him who came to visit him that day. Anything and everything I could think of, I told him. I think it was a way to keep my mind and my emotions positive, and I needed Bracey to be able to hear my voice and to know he was never going to be alone.

I stayed with Bracey like that, talking to him for nearly five days after his surgery. Once he came out of his coma, things started changing. Within seven days after his major surgery, he was able to come off the ventilator, and things started to progress, or at least I thought they would. Bracey developed a pneumothorax (air around the lungs). The doctors were quickly able to remove the air pocket with a syringe, but I could tell he was not progressing, and his oxygen-level numbers on the monitor proved it. They continued to drop, minute by minute, and then second by second. I was becoming very anxious, and quickly Bracey was surrounded by nurses and doctors. They had no choice but to reintubate (insert the breathing tube back into the trachea). He was fighting too hard to breathe.

Once intubated, he was able to rest his body. This was especially difficult for me. I had been so excited, thinking I was going to be able to hold him soon, and now I knew I would have to wait longer to once again hold my precious baby. His little body could not handle being moved around.

I prayed a prayer that night, and for the first time in my life, I felt as if God's hands were right on my shoulders, telling me everything would be okay. I knew without a doubt Bracey was going to recover completely and be a huge testimony to every single person he would come into contact with. God gave me an overwhelming amount of peace that night. I stayed with Bracey extralong that night before going to the Ronald McDonald House. I just held his hands and told him I knew everything was going to be all right. "Your little body just needs more time to heal, sweetheart. Take your time. I will be here every step of the way. God is watching over you, and you have angels all around you. You have amazing prayer warriors, family, and friends. When your body is ready, I will be here to hold you. I love you, Bracey!"

February 18, 2008—Twelve Days Old

Two days after being reintubated, the doctors decided it was time to start slowly turning his oxygen down. Bracey was becoming active and didn't want the breathing tube anymore. He would try to cry, and nothing would come out. I wanted so badly to hear his loud, strong cry. Bracey weaned off the ventilator like the fighter he is. At twelve days old, Bracey was in my arms! He still needed oxygen and still had over a dozen wires attached to him and in him, but he was cleared to be held!

As I mentioned before, I was obsessed with Bracey's monitor. I was always watching those numbers. I knew what each one of those numbers stood for and what range they should always be between. During his first two days off of the ventilator, those numbers would often drop, and the nurse would come over and move Bracey around a bit and adjust the tiny tube that was giving him oxygen through his nose, known as a nasal cannula. Torrey and I would huddle in the back and watch and pray as his numbers would go back up.

Later that second night, Torrey made me take a short break to go and get a bite to eat from the cafeteria. I never wanted to do that, but I knew I had to keep eating. When we got back, I noticed his numbers were a bit low again. They were right at the edge of the lower side of comfort. They never seemed to bounce back up like the other times. Instead, they were plummeting rapidly.

Within seconds, Bracey was surrounded by doctors and nurses. All of them were working hard to save our precious boy's life. Torrey and I knew right away this wasn't just going to be a little "nudging and all would be okay" type of event. This was very serious. Torrey and I were overwhelmed, and a nurse suggested we step out for a bit. I cried out to God like never before.

"God, how much more can Bracey take? Please allow this

to stop. Please just heal his body. Hasn't he had enough, Lord? Please just let me take his place, God. I will do anything if You just heal his body. I love You and am trusting You, God, but this is killing me! I know I may never know why You are doing this, but I will still trust you. Bracey is Yours, and he is in Your hands. Please just help us through this unbearable time."

Our incredible nurse, Misty, came and found us and said Bracey was comfortable again and stabilized. It was not until a few years later that I found out they had to bring Bracey back to life two times that night. Bracey's trachea and airway were swollen, so the doctors decided not to intubate again but to try a headed hood with him. This looks like a tent that allows 100 percent oxygen flow. Bracey responded very well to the headed hood, and we were still able to hold him for short increments at a time.

Two more days passed, and Bracey was becoming a very active little baby. He was determined to break free from that oxygen tent. Bracey was breathing 100 percent on his own and no longer needed the headed hood or a nasal cannula. I felt God's presence and knew this time Bracey was going to be okay. No more major setbacks. Bracey was a fighter from the moment of birth. Although his body was broken, Bracey was not going to let it stop him. He was determined to prove to the medical staff he was ready to become wire-free!

I knew Bracey being able to breathe 100 percent on his own was a huge step in recovery. The nurses and doctors kept reminding me Bracey still had a long way to go before he could be released from the hospital. After all, this five-pound baby did just have major surgery a couple weeks ago. Bracey was looking better and better. He was always being held by family, friends, nurses, and, of course, Torrey and me.

On day sixteen, Bracey was ready for his chest tube to be

removed. So, right there at his bedside, I watched as the doctors gently and quickly removed his chest tube. I was so ecstatic. One more tube gone! I knew exactly what this meant. It meant I no longer needed assistance from the nurses to hold my baby. I could swaddle him up and hold him any time I wanted.

The doctors mentioned Bracey was ready for an NG tube (feeding tube through his nose) so he could start receiving milk. I knew if he could start getting milk and responding well to it, the central line would be able to come out. It was as if his body had been craving this. His belly tolerated it well. He was so full of life. After two days of being fed through the NG tube, the doctors permitted Bracey to start bottle-feeding. Of course, it was only five cc's at a time, but at least it was something.

February 25, 2008—Nineteen Days Old

At nineteen days old, with tears streaming down my face, I was able to give Bracey his very first bottle. I think I had every emotion during this time. I was nervous he would not take it. I was anxious to see him finish it. I was overwhelmed with joy that I got to give him his first bottle. And like the little champ he is, he finished those five cc's within seconds. The doctors said if he continued to increase his feedings for the next twenty-four hours, we could remove his central line. And guess what? He got that nagging central line removed.

After his nurse removed his central line, she looked at me with a huge smile on her face and said, "Are you ready to give Bracey his first bath?" Yes! It was a precious time for me. He just kept staring at me. He never took his eyes off me, and I couldn't help but have the biggest grin on my face the entire time. I never wanted this bath to end. After his bath, he was able for the first time to wear real clothes. I put him in this cute little sleeper. He was the most adorable baby.

February 27, 2008—Twenty-One Days Old

Since Bracey was doing so well, the doctors decided it would be okay to order an occupational therapist to come and meet Bracey. Up to this point, we hadn't even worried about dealing with his hands. We knew they were not life-threatening and they could wait. Now that he was well on his way to being a NICU graduate, we knew we needed to speak with the therapist. She made splints for Bracey to wear during his resting time. She also showed us lots of stretches and things we could do to keep his hands in motion. She assured us none of this was painful. Bracey, unfortunately, did not care much for the splints. He did everything possible to get them off. At this point in his life, we decided the splints were not a high priority to us. We did continue to put them on him occasionally, but when they agitated him, they came right off.

Torrey and I made the decision it was time for Torrey to go back into work. His work was over an hour away from the hospital. We knew this would take a toll on Torrey, but he wanted to get back to work, even for just a few hours a day. He would get up very early and go sit with Bracey in the NICU and then come back in the evening and hold Bracey before bed.

At twenty-three days old, Bracey was able to have his NG tube removed. Torrey was at work, and I called him that morning and told him Bracey was about to become wireless. We were so excited. Now I knew it would only be days until Bracey would get to come home and start his life with us.

Bracey seemed to still have some rough times with the suck/swallow/breathe synchrony. His swallow tests always came back normal, no aspiration. The doctors assured us all babies have trouble with this the first few times they feed, but he would get it down.

March 6, 2008—Twenty-Nine Days Old

On day twenty-nine, as I was walking back up to the NICU, I began to talk with God.

"God, thank You so much for Your continued blessings in our lives. Thank You for Bracey. Thank You for giving Bracey such an amazing personality! Thank You for his sweet smile and strong will to fight for life. Thank You for being with us during the tough times in our lives and the wonderful times in our lives. God, today I am asking, if it is Your will, that You send us some encouraging news. I pray You will bless us today and continue to allow Bracey to take his bottles. Lord, You know no matter what, I will follow, obey, and love You."

As I was walking into Bracey's pod, it seemed as if the nurses and doctors were waiting for me. I immediately felt nervous, not sure what was going on. Bracey's doctor looked at me and said, "You can take Bracey home today." What? I couldn't believe it! Once again, this doctor got a huge hug from me. I hugged every nurse in sight. I then scooped up Bracey and danced around with him. I had to call Torrey right away to tell him the exciting news. He was going to bring his son home today!

"Oh, God, thank You! Your blessings are overwhelming today. I love You, Lord."

I was so excited and nervous to finally be able to bring Bracey home. There were about a hundred things I had to remember: doctors' follow-up appointments, measuring every cc of milk he drank, keeping him elevated at all times. The list went on. The nurses were great and had every appointment written down with the doctor's name, number, and address. His main nurse walked us down to the front doors, and I gave her such a huge, bittersweet hug. Misty requested to be assigned to Bracey every single time she was working. She was with Bracey during all of his ups and downs. She was the nurse who admitted Bracey the night he arrived at the hospital. I thank God for her. Had it not been for this incredible rock, Bracey would not be here. All of the nurses there were wonderful, and they all knew Bracey. Misty just had this special bond with him that can never be taken away.

I remember one night in particular I was not sleeping well at RMH, so I decided to visit Bracey. I got up to the NICU around four in the morning and found Misty playing with him. Bracey was a night owl and loved hanging out with his favorite nurse. She was very protective of him. It was not easy telling Misty goodbye; however, we still keep in touch with her, even to this day. We love you, Misty, and thank you for your awesome dedication to helping heal precious babies every day.

On March 6, 2008, we were finally home as a family. My mom was able to stay with us for the first week. It was wonderful having her with us. She and my sister had been very instrumental to us, as they stayed many days with us at the Ronald McDonald House. They kept our laundry and room very clean. We were blessed to be able to have a large room with two beds so they could stay. It was comforting coming back to my room each evening and never feeling alone.

March 6, 2008—One Month Old

His first week at home was filled with visitors and doctors' appointments. Of course, they were all on different days, and they were all in Chicago, an hour away from us. The first of Bracey's four doctors' appointments was with a neurosurgeon. Bracey had developed a little bit of fluid on his brain during his stay at the NICU. They had done an MRI on his brain prior to us leaving the hospital, and we were headed back to get the results. The results were interesting.

The doctor said Bracey had microcephaly. All of the parts of his brain were there and had developed correctly. The only problem was his brain was very tiny. He showed us pictures of a normal infant's brain and how it fills up the entire head. Then he showed us pictures of Bracey's brain. It only filled up about half of his head. "What does this mean?" I asked. Basically, it meant nothing needed to be done for Bracey. He has a very small brain. It could mean he may have trouble learning, and things may take him longer to accomplish, but, in reality, his brain is healthy and functioning perfectly. That was a great outcome, and we were happy with those results.

It was so incredibly wonderful to be home with Bracey. He was still a noisy eater, and I shared my concern often with the doctor about how he sounded wheezy during his bottles. The first week, I was told to only give him three ounces every three hours, and after eight swallows, I was to take the bottle out for about a minute to give him a break. His feedings took almost an hour. We tried this for a few days to see if it would help make him slow down and take breaths.

After a few days of feeding like this, I knew something was wrong. He was not getting better. In fact, if it was possible, I felt as if he was getting worse. He would turn a bit grayish blue and wheeze quite loudly. I called the doctor, and he scheduled a barium swallow test for Bracey, as the doctor thought maybe there was some constriction at the sight of surgery. I explained he also turned grayish blue when he got upset. The barium test was scheduled for March 14.

On March 18, we got the test results back, and the doctor said Bracey had tracheomalacia and would grow out of it. Tracheomalacia is when the cartilage in the trachea has not developed properly, and the trachea becomes floppy and essentially collapses. The doctor told us to just keep doing what we were doing, and as he gained weight, his trachea would strengthen, and he would quickly grow out of this.

So, for the next week, we continued giving him small amounts of milk at a time and giving him breaks so he could breathe. I was not seeing any improvement. I was getting concerned because my son was not getting better and was becoming agitated during his bottle feedings.

This was not right. I called the doctor again, and I was sure by now he was thinking I was becoming a paranoid mother. He just had his nurse assure me Bracey would be fine and would grow out of this. It just would take time. I asked how long it should take, because this did not seem safe or healthy for my baby. The doctor again assured me this was completely normal and that it could take a couple months for a new baby with tracheomalacia to heal. I thought to myself, *I do not agree*, but I didn't know what else to do.

He was the doctor, and he was supposed to know the medical side of Bracey's body. I am the mother, and maybe my emotions were getting the best of me. Bracey was in God's hands, and God had brought him this far. I knew God would continue to protect him.

"Dear Lord, please help Bracey learn how to suck/swallow/breathe. Lord, he needs to gain weight so he can strengthen his trachea. Lord, please heal his precious body. Thank You for watching over my son and for never leaving us. I love You, Lord."

Easter weekend was upon us, and we had decided to go visit family and show Bracey off to many of our friends and family down near Muncie, Indiana. Easter came early that year. It landed on March 23. This is the one Easter weekend neither Torrey nor I will ever forget. It encompassed, by far, one of the worst moments in my life.

We were at my parents' house in Daleville, Indiana, on March 21. My sister, her husband, and their young son were there as well. It was three thirty in the morning, and everyone was sound asleep. Bracey was waking up for his feeding. I went and got his three-ounce bottle ready. I came back to our room and cuddled Bracey as he started taking his first few swallows of the bottle. No problem. He was, of course, wheezy, but that was Bracey's normal. He took a break, and I offered his second set of swallows of milk. He started to become agitated, and then he just stopped.

Not even a single sound. It was as if he had just completely fallen asleep, except I could not hear him. I flipped on the light and screamed, "Torrey! He's not breathing! He's not breathing!" I am sure my scream woke the entire house.

Torrey grabbed Bracey out of my arms and immediately began CPR on our lifeless, completely gray baby. I called 911, my mom called my dad, who was working, and my sister and her husband were at the foot of our bed, down on their knees, praying to

God. Everything was so surreal and happened so quickly. Torrey continued his CPR for about three minutes. We finally heard Bracey make a tiny squeak—and then nothing again. Torrey continued his CPR. I heard the ambulance and police sirens. They were at our house within minutes. Just as the EMTs were running into our house, Bracey let out a huge cry. It was the best cry I have ever heard.

The EMTs took Bracey and started working on him, giving him much-needed oxygen and checking his vitals. After fifteen minutes of oxygen, Bracey was sound asleep. It was as if nothing had ever happened. While he slept in Torrey's arms, we stood around and talked to the EMTs and the police, who were all very curious about Bracey's condition. They had never seen anyone with Bracey's condition. We gave them the short version of what Bracey's condition entailed. They had never heard of VACTERL association before. They were very intrigued as we shared Bracey's story with them.

They gave us the option to take Bracey to the hospital, but we decided he was okay and we would keep him home. I was on edge for the next few hours. I was so nervous about his next feeding. But it had to come, and Bracey did well. He was still very wheezy and agitated during his next feeding, but he never stopped breathing.

Whew, I felt like a weight had lifted off my shoulders. I was able to get a hold of his doctor, and he said that since it was a weekend, and a holiday weekend at that, if we felt like Bracey needed to be seen, we could take him to the local hospital. This was not the most encouraging news to us, so we just continued our day. Part of me wondered if I was just so tired that I forgot to take the bottle out after eight swallows or if Bracey was just so tired that he forgot to breathe. So many unanswered questions continued to linger in my head. Why couldn't I get a single clear answer about Bracey? This surely wasn't normal.

Later that afternoon, I, along with my mother, sister, and Bracey, decided to go shopping. This was the first time Bracey had been out in a public store. I kept him well bundled and in his car seat most of the time. While shopping, I knew he was getting fussy and needed a bottle. I sat down on a bench and began his slow, long feeding. During his very first couple of swallows, I noticed he was starting to become more agitated than normal. I stopped feeding right away and gave him a few minutes. He was getting upset because he was hungry. He was wheezing terribly, and he sounded like he was struggling a lot to exhale.

I was very nervous and just asked God to quickly calm him down so he could take a breath. Bracey, almost instantly, stopped crying and was calm again. I hurried to find my mom and sister and told them we needed to get home. I told Torrey about it, and we prayed ... a lot.

"Lord, we do not want to send him back to the hospital. We just got out of the hospital, and we want to start a normal life with our baby. Lord, what do You want us to do? If Bracey needs to be put in the hospital, please just give us peace about this. Please help us not to be selfish with Bracey. Lord, we gave Bracey to You the minute we found out we were pregnant. If You want him, You can have him. Please just show us what we need to do. We trust You, Lord."

We both knew, almost instantly, we needed to get Bracey into a hospital. We called the on-call doctor in Chicago and asked where we should go. We told him Bracey needed help. The doctor arranged with a hospital nearby Indianapolis for us to take Bracey there. So, at eleven o'clock that night, we kissed my parents goodbye, and my sister and her husband drove us to the hospital.

I thought the worst part was behind us, but God knew it wasn't. Yes, the NICU had been extremely difficult and full of emotional roller coasters, but with God's help, we made it through. We would make it through this too.

March 22, 2008—Six and a Half Weeks Old

The next seventy-two hours were physically and emotionally awful. Once admitted to the hospital, the first thing they did was put two IVs into Bracey's head. The nurses asked us to leave while they did this. We stepped out of the room and heard the most torturous cries. My heart was breaking. Just twelve hours ago, we were all home as a family, having a great time. "God, what is going on?"

After the nurses were done, I ran in his room and swept him up into my arms. "I'm so sorry, Bracey," I kept repeating in his ear. A couple of doctors came in and asked about his story. We shared it, hoping for answers. No answers came. Torrey even drew one of the doctors a picture of Bracey's initial tracheoesophageal fistula so they could get a better understanding of his insides.

After about three hours of being in our holding room, the doctor came in and said he would have to put us in a permanent room until he was able to get more information from Bracey's doctor in Chicago. That room, however, would not be ready for many hours, so we waited in the emergency room for nine hours. Of course, Bracey's doctor was not going to be reachable until Tuesday morning. So, at six o'clock on Easter Sunday morning, we were placed in a small joint room. Bracey had lost a lot of weight during the last few days, so the doctor in Indy (Indianapolis,

Indiana) ordered an NG tube so he could eat. Nothing was allowed in his mouth until his doctor up in Chicago could assess him.

For two and a half very long days, we just sat in that room. The doctors would not do any tests, or even touch Bracey, because he was not their patient. The nurses treated us as if we were just wasting a bed. They were only ordered to keep his IV open and to turn on his NG pump when he was ready to eat.

It was a completely different world at this hospital. We felt like we were just a number, borrowing a bed until Tuesday. It was terrible. They gave us two hard chairs. No couches, no beds, nothing comfortable. The other child we were sharing the room with seemed to cry the entire time we were there. Torrey and I were both so extremely exhausted. We sat the entire time, holding Bracey and praying we could soon leave. The only nice thing about the situation was many of our family members lived near Muncie, about forty-five minutes away, and were able to visit us.

Finally, after seventy-two long, sleepless hours, Tuesday morning came, and we were ready to get some answers. The doctor came in and said the doctors in Chicago wanted Bracey to return to the hospital. Next thing we knew, we were handed discharge papers and sent on our way to drive back up to Chicago with our child. That was it; no transportation team was offered to take Bracey up to Chicago. We were so upset. We could have driven to Chicago on Sunday had we known this hospital was going to be such a terrible, pointless place for my baby. I have never been so ready to leave a place more than that hospital.

We were quickly admitted back into the hospital in Chicago. It was just like going home. Everything was familiar. The only sad thing was we could not be back in the NICU with our amazing nurses. However, we had our own room, and we met some other wonderful nurses. There were fantastic child life specialists who made sure we had anything we needed (i.e., movies, cafeteria tickets, etc.). They made sure we knew our way around the hospital and where the lounge was located for our floor. Words could not express how happy we were to be back in Chicago.

March 25, 2008—Seven Weeks Old

The first day there was mostly a day of meeting with doctors and nurses and getting tests scheduled for the next few days. Although we had so many unanswered questions, we knew Bracey would get the best possible care. We had a beautiful room with a pull-out couch and a La-Z-Boy, and by that time, that's all we wanted … rest.

His doctors had scheduled multiple tests over the next few days. The first was another barium swallow test and then a motility test, which records movement and pressures of the esophagus. So, on Wednesday, day five of being in a hospital, we were finally doing tests. These first two tests came back completely normal. On one hand, we gave a sigh of relief because he was not aspirating while eating, but on the other hand, we still had no answers. Late that afternoon, Bracey's head doctor came in our room and spent almost two hours with us. He was so patient and tried to answer our questions. He was able to relieve some of our frustrations at not knowing and helped us feel confident we would find the reason for Bracey's episodes. He promised, although it could take a few days, we would not have to leave the hospital without answers. That night, we slept the best we had in over a week. (Well, as great as one can sleep in a hospital.) Just knowing we were in a place that cared about our child and was determined to figure out what was going on inside of Bracey's body gave us such peace and assurance.

Thursday came, and Bracey was scheduled for an EEG. This was a long test. They wanted to rule out seizures as a possible cause for Bracey to stop breathing. This test came back normal. Following those results, the doctor ordered another test, which would take place on Friday. This test was an esophageal gram. It would determine if there were possibly any more fistulas (an abnormal connection or passageway between the esophagus and trachea that should not connect). This test also came back normal. We were running low on energy and hope.

The only wonderful thing about these last six days was that Bracey was a champ! He very rarely cried, and he slept a lot. He was very happy to just be cuddled.

On day six, we were surprised by our very favorite nurse from the NICU, Misty. She came early one morning and brought Bracey a gift bag. It was so wonderful to see her. That visit truly brightened our day.

Since the esophageal gram came back normal, the doctor had yet another test he wanted to order. This one was a bit trickier and couldn't be done until Tuesday. Ugh, what in the world were we supposed to do until Tuesday? We asked the doctor if it would be possible for us to take Bracey home for the weekend and come back Monday. He said that might be a possibility and left the room. Having some hope we would get to go home after another week of being in the hospital was exciting. I went ahead and started packing as if the doctor had already said yes.

When the doctor came back in the room, he said he thought it would be good for us to go home and be a family for the weekend. He was going to have a nurse teach us how to use the NG tube pump, and she would take the IV out of his head. Yes! At that point, we would have done anything to get to take Bracey home for the weekend. It seemed that as long as he was on the NG, he did great. He hadn't stopped breathing since he was able to take food through the NG tube. It was like, as long as he didn't have to swallow, he had no problems.

March 28, 2008—Eight Weeks Old

Aww, being home was such a relief. Having an NG tube was nerve-racking at times. We had to daily change the tape holding the tube to Bracey's face because he was getting terrible sores from it. Every day since he had it put in, the nurses would rotate the tube so it wasn't resting on the same cheek. This was tough because Bracey would pull on it, and I feared it would come out. If it came out, we would have to go the local ER to have it put back in. Because of Bracey's previous surgery, his esophagus was very narrow, and only a professional would be able to get it back in. So, we were very cautious with his tube.

I must take a moment to praise Bracey. All the way up to this point, he has been a brave fighter. He was only two months old, and he had lived most of his life in the hospital, but he was such an encouraging little baby. He was so strong. He rarely cried. He was, and is, my definition of a miracle. He has beaten death more than once. He had been through a major surgery with multiple complications during the recovery. He was not allowed to take bottles and had to be fed through his nose. Through all of this, Bracey was still happy. He was content. When he slept, he looked so peaceful, and when he was awake, he was content and smiling.

Our weekend home went by too fast. It was a great couple of

days full of family and visitors. It gave us a chance to catch up on some needed rest and to pack for the following week. We did not know what the week would hold for us, but we knew God was in control and He would take care of Bracey.

Monday afternoon, we were back in the hospital. The hospital had another wonderful room ready for us. Bracey needed to have an IV put in. This IV turned out to be a nightmare. Now that he was getting older, the veins in his head were not as easy to access, so they had to use the foot. Bracey did not like this IV one bit.

Four hours went by, and Bracey was still crying from the IV. Torrey asked the nurse for Tylenol for Bracey to see if it would help with his pain, but she told us he was a baby and babies cry. This did not make us happy. She had no clue who Bracey was. This was not normal for our baby. Bracey rarely cried. To us, his parents, he was obviously in pain. After we explained this was not normal for our child, she agreed to ask the doctor if Bracey could have some Tylenol. Within minutes of Bracey getting Tylenol through his IV, he was completely calm and fell asleep. This just proved we knew our baby and would continue to fight for the absolute best care for Bracey.

April 1, 2008—Two Months Old

The following day after being back in the hospital, Bracey had a bronchial scope. This is where they place a tiny camera down his trachea via the nose and look for floppiness of the trachea while he is taking a bottle. I did not want to do this test. I was afraid of what could happen during this test, but the doctors assured us everything would be okay and there would be doctors and nurses on standby should anything happen.

As the test began, I reluctantly started giving him his bottle. This was the first time he'd had a bottle since March 22. Bracey started taking swallows, and the wheezing started instantly. I said we needed to stop this test, but they insisted he was doing great and to keep going. I continued giving him the bottle, and he started getting agitated. I heard his monitor going off, and he was starting to turn blue. I stopped giving the bottle and yelled for someone to help. They grabbed Bracey quickly and began to give him oxygen.

Within seconds, Bracey was unresponsive and lifeless. I could not believe this was happening again. They attached a mouthpiece with a bag and placed it over Bracey's mouth and began squeezing it, which gave Bracey air as they started chest compressions. I was inconsolable and refused to leave the room.

It took Bracey four and a half minutes before he was able to breathe again. After they felt like Bracey was stable, they gave him back to me and wheeled us back to our room. Bracey slept for hours. I told Torrey he was not allowed to leave me for work tomorrow because I needed him with me. I had been enduring all these tests alone with Bracey, and I was physically, emotionally, and spiritually drained. Today's events threw me over the edge.

I was beginning to get mad at everyone and everything. I was mad at Torrey for leaving me alone that day. I was mad at the technician who would not stop when I said Bracey had had enough. I was mad at the doctors for running Bracey through test after test and not having any answers for us. I was mad we had been living in the hospital for two months. I was mad I couldn't give my baby a bottle, let alone nurse him. I was mad I was stuck in a room all day, hours away from family and friends. I was mad we couldn't have a normal life. I was mad Bracey was not healthy. I was mad God would allow someone so precious and innocent to go through such pain and misery. The only thing that carried me through was Bracey being in my arms and breathing steadily.

I am sure at that moment Satan was cheering because he thought he had finally broken me. No, Satan did not break me. Was I upset and confused with God? Yes, absolutely. But what Christian goes through their entire life never being confused as to what God was trying to teach them? I was mad at this entire situation, and I just wanted answers.

His test results from the scope came back normal. The doctors were all baffled and decided this was just something Bracey would need to grow out of. There was nothing else they could do, since they could not find a specific cause for these episodes. So, on April 3, we were sent home. Bracey was still on NG feedings and would continue with these feeds for a couple more weeks to allow his body to get bigger and stronger. We sighed yet again, packed up our things, and headed home without clear answers.

The next few weeks were filled with wonderful times, stressful times, and exhausting times. Bracey had a checkup in Chicago once a week, and a nurse came to the house twice a week to change out Bracey's NG tube and to take his vitals. The nurse always seemed to have a hundred questions. Although I understood how to change out the NG tube, Bracey's esophagus was not structured like a normal esophagus, so the doctor wanted the nurse to do these changes. I really did appreciate the nurse coming out. It was a lot of work to pack him up along with all of his medical equipment. I rarely took him out of the house. We spent most of our days hanging out at home. Bracey had begun therapy on his hands twice a week. These sessions mainly consisted of stretching his hands to make sure they didn't stiffen.

During these weeks, Bracey still wheezed from time to time when he was crying, but he enjoyed his pacifier, so we were able to use this most of the time to help calm him down. The wheezing sounds always made me nervous and sad—nervous because those were always the sounds Bracey made just before he stopped breathing, and sad because I knew as long as he still wheezed, he would probably not be able to tolerate a bottle.

Bracey had a doctor's appointment on April 16, and the doctor scheduled for Bracey to be admitted to the hospital on April 28 to be observed for a twenty-four-hour period of bottle feedings. If he passed all of those feedings with no drop in his oxygen level, then the NG tube would come out, and we could resume bottle-feeding. If he could not handle the bottle feedings, then Bracey would need a G-tube. A G-tube is a long-term solution for feeding. He would be fed through a tube directly into his stomach. The surgery and recovery time would be about a week at the hospital. I was praying Bracey could take a bottle, but I was also praying for peace if he needed a G-tube.

April 19, 2008—Two Months Old

This morning turned into one of the absolute toughest mornings I have ever had. I was bathing Bracey and getting him ready for the day. My parents were coming up for a visit. Torrey was off running an errand for his job. I had just lifted Bracey out of the tub and was drying him off when he started to get fussy. Like most babies, he was probably just cold and wanted to be warm again. He continued to get fussier and was wheezing loudly. I called Torrey while trying to comfort Bracey and asked him when he would be home.

Bracey was getting more upset, and I could not calm him down this time. I was trying to stay calm, but I was nervous. While I was still on the phone with Torrey, Bracey started gasping for air and turning gray. Torrey yelled at me to hang up and call 911. Bracey stopped breathing and was limp in my arms.

As I held onto my lifeless baby, I dialed 911. I began CPR while waiting for the operator. Once the operator got on the line, I felt as if she had a million questions. I told her to just send the paramedics, and I continued CPR. I gave over ten breaths before I heard a little noise come out of my blue, lifeless baby. There was a noise and then nothing again. I continued giving him little breaths and chest compressions. Eight minutes went by, and a police officer ran into my living room, where I was still giving Bracey breaths. The officer took over, and the paramedics were there almost immediately afterward.

He finally let out a loud cry just as the paramedics came into the house. Bracey was very blue still and needed oxygen. The paramedics wasted no time in giving him oxygen. Within minutes, we were in the ambulance, headed to the local hospital. Bracey's oxygen level was very low.

As I was holding him, he finally began calming down. I could hear a lot of junk in Bracey's windpipe, and I asked if he could be suctioned out. The paramedic gave me a little baby suction, and I was able to suction him out. Within seconds of being suctioned out, Bracey was breathing at 100 percent again.

Torrey met us as we were pulling into the ER. I was pretty shaken up, and Bracey was resting in my arms. We explained everything to the ER doctors, and they ran some precautionary tests, which, as usual for Bracey, all came back fine. We were in the hospital for about three hours.

While we were there, my brother-in-law, Tom, came to visit and to pray with us. I was holding Bracey and looked up at Tom and said, "I am so tired. I can't do this anymore. Why is God doing this?" Tom, with tears in his eyes, held my hand and prayed with me.

I was reminded that when we are overwhelmed and feel like we cannot bear it anymore, God will bear it for us. We must keep our faith in knowing that, although we seem overwhelmed and alone, with unanswered questions, God knows why, and God will help us through those times. I knew God would get our child through this and would get us through it as well.

We must continue to trust in Him and give it all completely to Him. There are so many times when I want to just fix it all, and I forget God is in control. God is the ultimate healer, and He has a purpose. His timing is perfect, not mine. Bracey is in God's hands, and God will protect him. God does not promise there will never be struggles, pain, sorrow, or questions. He just promises He will never leave us and will help us through these times. I must give it all to Him and rely on Him for peace and comfort. That day was definitely a huge turning point for me.

On April 28, we headed back to the hospital for yet another swallow study. We told them if Bracey showed any signs of distress, we would *not* allow the procedure to continue. And, of course, Bracey did not finish the procedure because his oxygen levels started dropping, and he began wheezing. With a huge sigh, we went back to our room and waited to meet with the doctors. Later that afternoon, we met with Bracey's main doctor and a gastroenterologist. They took a great deal of time in explaining we were out of options and Bracey needed a G-tube. We were saddened but knew this was what Bracey needed to survive. He could not keep eating through an NG tube. They scheduled his surgery for May 1.

May 1, 2008—Just about Three Months

The morning of May 1 weighed heavy on my heart. I was full of mixed emotions. Part of me felt like we gave up on finding answers for Bracey, and the other part of me knew that Bracey couldn't continue on the NG tube and needed the G-tube placement for a more permanent solution. I hated that Bracey had to have another surgery and spend more time in the hospital. The neurosurgeon wanted to get another MRI on his brain to see if the fluid had decreased, so the doctors decided to do that on the same day. We were able to be with Bracey and hold his hands at the beginning of the MRI, while the anesthesiologist put him under sedation.

About two and half hours into the MRI, a nurse came out and said that he was finished with the MRI, and the G-tube placement was beginning. The doctors kept him heavily sedated for the next twenty-four hours. During his G-tube surgery, the doctor also did a bronchoscope, which showed his tracheomalacia but no other fistulas. The doctors were not concerned with his tracheomalacia and told us he would grow out of it as his trachea got stronger. The MRI showed the abundance of fluid on his brain at birth was gone, so he did not need a shunt put in.

That evening, Bracey needed a second IV. They wanted another access point in case one went bad; they could quickly get to another one. So, they put an IV in Bracey's neck. Bracey, still heavily sedated, felt it and squirmed a lot—so much he accidentally pulled his breathing tube out a little bit. The nurse finished her IV and then began trying to get his tube back in place. Meanwhile, Bracey was becoming more agitated. His oxygen level dropped quickly, and within seconds, doctors and nurses were being called to our room. Because Bracey was heavily sedated, he was unable to breathe without his ventilator.

It took the doctors and nurses twenty-five minutes to replace his tube. Nurses were bagging him and doing chest compressions, while the doctors had to take the tube out and replace it.

It was so surreal that this was happening. Bracey was in a very delicate situation. Having just undergone G-tube surgery, he was not supposed to be moved around much.

Two hours after that drama, I was watching Bracey because he still seemed a bit agitated and was trying to cry. I thought this was weird because the doctor told us they were going to place Bracey in a coma for the next twenty-four hours to let his body heal. He should not be moving around and trying to cry. I was holding his hand and trying to talk calmly to him when I noticed a great deal of swelling at the sight of his neck IV.

Torrey called for the nurse and showed her the IV. The nurse was immediately apologetic and had another nurse come in with her. Bracey's IV was not in his vein. It was just in his neck, and the meds he was receiving to keep him asleep were just going into his neck, causing a buildup of the fluids. The nurse quickly removed his IV completely and moved his meds to his other IV, which was in his head. Within almost seconds of Bracey getting the meds through his other IV, he was asleep.

I was terribly upset. My faith in our medical staff was quickly failing. I felt like they could not tell us what was going on with our son. The only answer they had for us was a G-tube. *Well,* I thought, *how in the world is this G-tube going to keep my baby alive?*

Is this going to keep him breathing? No! I understand Bracey needs to eat, but he also needs to breathe, and not a single person can tell me why he stops breathing. I wanted answers they could not give. I truly believe they did not know what was causing Bracey's inability to breathe. All of the tests came back normal, so they just kept saying, "He will grow out of it." Torrey and I were so naïve we believed them. They were, after all, the educated ones, right?

May 7, 2008

Ten days after being in the hospital, Bracey was finally ready to come home again. Our house was filled with medical technicians coming in and out all afternoon. By the end of the day, our house looked like our hospital room: machines everywhere, oxygen tanks, IV bags, and poles. Bracey was on an oxygen monitor around the clock. We had a large oxygen tank in the living room and two small ones we could carry with us. His food pump was hooked onto an IV pole. During the first three weeks after his G-tube surgery, he had to be fed through this rubber tube that was coming out of his stomach. This rubber tube had to stay upright during his feedings, and when he wasn't feeding, we had to shut it off with a clip like you would use for a bag of chips. If it did not get clipped correctly, then his milk would leak back out.

You can probably imagine how often Bracey and I left the house. Not very often. Torrey was still working every day, and I quickly realized I could not handle this on my own. We had the option of Bracey staying at a hospice, but I did not want that for my baby. While I had been trained how to do everything, I just did not want to be alone. Graciously, my mom took short leave from her job and came to be with me during the week. She went back home on the weekends, when Torrey was able to be with Bracey and me. I knew she could not do this forever, and I would soon need to be able to take care of Bracey on my own. But, for now, it was a huge comfort to know I never had to be alone.

May 21 came, and Bracey was ready to get his Mic-key. This was basically a permanent button that was inserted into his stomach, making it very easy for him to eat. Finally, that large, messy, rubber tube was ready to be replaced. This was a simple procedure, done in the doctor's office, but it was uncomfortable for Bracey. Having this little button now meant so much. His feedings were much easier, he was able to take a bath, and he was finally able to have tummy time.

Coming home from the doctor's office that day, I felt so relieved. The last three weeks had been terrible, but we were now on our way to a healthy baby boy. Sure, he would have to eat through his stomach instead of his mouth, but he was growing and happy. I felt like things were looking up.

We began noticing a pattern with Bracey. It seemed like just as things were calmed down, Bracey would have an episode. That evening, Bracey did just that. He was a bit fussy the entire afternoon after receiving his new Mic-key. I am sure he was just tender from the pushing and tugging of the placement of the Mic-key. Later that evening, he really began to get agitated. Even between me, Torrey, and my mom, we were unable to calm him down. This was not typical Bracey. He was usually very easy to settle down.

Around nine o'clock that night, his oxygen monitor went off. We watched it and stayed as calm as possible; however, as Bracey continued to cry, the numbers on his monitor continued to drop. The added oxygen we gave him was not helping, and he was not calming down. His numbers were dropping quickly. I grabbed the phone and called 911. Bracey's oxygen was around 40 percent when the EMTs showed up. They quickly took us to the local hospital. During the ride to the hospital, Bracey finally began to calm down and was breathing great on his own by the time we made it to the hospital. They kept Bracey for a couple hours for observation and then sent us home.

Still, nobody could explain why Bracey's oxygen levels would randomly go down. His main doctors could not tell us. The ER doctors could not tell us. We were told by all of his doctors to just keep Bracey calm as much as possible. *Sure*, I thought, *no problem! Keep an infant from crying, easy peasy.*

May 23, 2008—Three and a Half Months Old

It was time for Mom to head back home. It was tough telling her goodbye. When she drove away, I felt all alone. I hadn't worried about laundry, groceries, dinners, and so on. Those last few weeks, I had peace, knowing someone was with me at all times. I knew it was unfair of me to ask her or anyone to be with me 24-7.

I felt like we lived on eggshells. We were always on edge anytime Bracey got upset, wondering if this would be the time God took him home. I was completely overwhelmed and felt a crushing accountability as Torrey would go to work and Bracey's life became solely my responsibility. I could not handle this on my own anymore. I was afraid of being at home alone with my own baby. My heart was so heavy. What kind of a mother is afraid to be alone with her baby? I hated that I felt like this. I just couldn't bear the thought of ever being alone with Bracey in case he stopped breathing again. It is the worst feeling in the world. Feelings of loneliness, helplessness, and failure all fell upon me. I prayed many hours, asking God to give me peace.

A couple of days went by, and I knew what Bracey and I needed. When I finally expressed all of my feelings to Torrey, we both agreed it was time to move in with my parents.

I knew this meant leaving our doctors in Chicago and getting new ones in Indianapolis. It also meant Torrey would have to quit his job and grad school. This was not an easy decision, and it was not made lightly. But, at this point in our lives, nothing was more important than keeping Bracey alive.

Once everyone involved was on board, I felt immense relief. It all happened very quickly, as our lease was up for renewal at the end of the month. So, within a week of our decision, we were packed up and moving to my parents' house in Daleville, Indiana. What an incredible feeling it was just knowing Bracey and I would never have to be alone.

Things were calming down for us as we started a new life in Daleville. God provided a couple of jobs for Torrey, and we found an amazing pediatric doctor right away. He was able to set up appointments with specialists at a children's hospital in Indianapolis. We knew right away that Bracey was in good hands. It was difficult to leave Chicago because we had been through so much with all of his doctors there, but we also were happy to try a new, fresh set of doctors. We had never received a real diagnosis of Bracey's dropping oxygen levels, and we were ready for new, fresh minds to assess Bracey.

June 25, 2008

The first doctor we were able to see was a GI doctor. She took him off one medicine his previous pediatrician had placed him on and added a different one. She also explained Bracey had developed a granuloma around his G-tube. This is basically an infection causing the skin around his G-tube to bubble up, and it looked terribly painful. She put him on another medicine to heal his infection. She fell in love with Bracey instantly, and we felt great relief with this new doctor.

As the next month went by, Bracey began to roll over and giggle and laugh at specific things. We could tell his tracheomalacia was not getting any better because when he would laugh, just like when he cried, he would have trouble breathing. So, we had to limit how much we could let him laugh. He still giggled a lot, but we tried to make sure he never had huge belly laughs.

As time passed, we learned the things you could and could not do with Bracey. He was five months old and was doing pretty well for Bracey. We went an entire month without any episodes. He was just so content lying on his play mat. God truly gave Bracey an amazing personality. We knew from the beginning Bracey was a fighter. But God had also given him an amazing ability to light up any room he was in. Anyone who met Bracey fell in love with him. His joy was just so contagious.

Whenever we relaxed and thought Bracey was doing incredibly well was the moment Bracey would have a setback.

July 13, 2008—Five Months

On what started as a normal day for us, Bracey's G-tube fell out. This was something new to us, and we did not know what to do. Since it was a Sunday, we called the on-call doctor at his GI clinic. The doctor told us to go to the ER, and they could put a new one in. The following week, our own doctor would be able to give us an extra Mic-key button and show us how to replace it ourselves if it ever came out again.

So, off to the local ER we went. Bracey was still happy, considering he had now missed a meal. We arrived at the ER around five o'clock in the evening (about an hour after it came out). After going through Bracey's complete medical history, they were ready to put in another Mic-key button. The nurse came in with a Mic-key, and I saw it did not look like the original that had fallen out. I showed her the original Mic-key, and she said they did not carry them that small at this hospital. I asked her, "Don't you have a NICU here?" I assumed the NICU would have supplies like this. She left the room to check, only to return saying the NICU didn't carry that size either. She opened the new, larger Mic-key, and I quickly said, "I don't think you should put something that's bigger than the opening in it." I did not want that large Mic-key button shoved into my son's belly. I was cringing in pain just thinking about it. She left the room once again and came back with a doctor. The doctor suggested they place a small tube in the opening just to keep it open, and we would need to drive to Indy to have the right size put in.

Okay, I thought, *we should have just gone straight to our hospital in Indy.* Trust me, from that point on, if Bracey ever needed to go to the ER, we went straight to *his* hospital. We never imagined it would be such an ordeal to replace a Mic-key. At seven o'clock, now three hours after the Mic-key fell out, the nurse came in to insert a small tube to ensure the opening stayed open. It was obvious the G-tube site was already closing. Torrey and I held Bracey down as the nurse inserted the tube. She was pushing hard, and we all heard a pop. Bracey immediately began to scream and cry. My heart shattered. We had waited too long. We should have just put that tube in right away while decisions were being made about what to do.

Bracey would not calm down. This was definitely a cry of pain and hurt rather than just his fussy, mad cry. I tried everything I could think of to calm him while they did paperwork to discharge us to head to Indy. When we finally headed out to our car, Bracey seemed to be asleep, so I placed him in his car seat. Within seconds, he was screaming again, and we knew he was going to stop breathing. He was wheezing and turning gray.

Torrey and I ran back in with him and basically tore through the doors to the ER rooms, yelling for a doctor to help us. It was just like in the medical shows when you see a person barging into the ER, carrying someone, and they are desperate for any doctor to help them. Well, that was us. We needed the doctors to realize Bracey was about to stop breathing. He needed oxygen and to be suctioned out immediately.

They moved quickly and were able to get him suctioned out and get him much-needed oxygen. In light of this mini episode, the doctors now did not feel comfortable with sending Bracey to Indy unless it was by ambulance. So, we waited some more while they made arrangements to transport us to our hospital in Indy. Bracey was still fussy, but moments after being moved in the ambulance, he was fast asleep. He woke up once, very unhappily (I'm sure from pain and hunger). The EMT turned up his oxygen and suctioned him out. Bracey calmed back down and rested until we got there.

Once we were in the wonderful hands of our favorite hospital, I was at peace. They were so wonderful and helped make it very easy for Bracey as they placed a new Mic-key in his opening. As soon as the Mic-key was in, they gave Bracey medicine to help with the pain, and we were able to feed him.

They brought in a pump and milk for Bracey. They offered snacks and drinks for Torrey and me. His doctor wanted to monitor him for a few hours to make sure he was feeding okay and his pain was gone.

They had to suction him out again while we were there. Bracey doesn't ever like these suctions, as you have to stick a tube down his throat to get all of the phlegm. But his oxygen levels always go way up after a suctioning.

The doctor gave us a Mic-key to have at home and showed us how to insert it and remove it if we ever needed. We were so grateful to be in such good hands. At one thirty in the morning, we were sent home. Thankfully, my dad came to pick us up, as we had left our car back at the first hospital.

During the next month, Bracey continued to struggle daily with his breathing. His wheezing was getting worse. When I say wheezing, I mean it sounded like someone who has a tight chest and is working very hard to breathe. This was Bracey every single day. I could tell it was getting worse because now when his belly was full, he would get even louder. I was so sleep deprived and living on edge. I just sat next to him, watching and listening to him. I felt like I could not leave his side for fear he would stop breathing.

August 12, 2008—Six Months Old

August came, and Bracey reached six months old. August was life-changing for Bracey. After six months of struggling to keep Bracey alive and breathing, God brought an angel into our lives in the form of a pediatric pulmonologist from the hospital in Indianapolis.

The minute she stepped into our exam room, I knew she was sent from God. She had this amazing enthusiasm and joy on her face. She instantly made a connection with Bracey that no other doctor had ever made. She showed us an outpouring of kindness and caring for our son. Bracey was not just a chart of medical problems. He was a little baby boy who desperately needed help.

She sat and listened intently as I explained *everything* that had happened in the last six months. She had tears in her eyes. She was listening to me and showed complete sympathy for us. She was so saddened we had not been referred to her before now. She went on and asked if she could examine Bracey.

She listened to his chest not even five seconds and then stopped and looked at me with tears in her eyes. She said, "I cannot believe Bracey has not had a tracheotomy." She stopped her exam immediately and brought in a respiratory therapist to do two breathing treatments on him before she continued her exam. The treatments took about fifteen minutes. After the treatments, our doctor came back in. She had reviewed all of his reports, tests, procedures, and surgeries from all of his other doctors.

She assured us his condition was quite serious and needed immediate aggressive action. I was all ears. I was ready for action after six months of just reacting. She went on to assure us Bracey would never grow out of this. He has tracheomalacia. Tracheomalacia is when the cartilage in the trachea has not developed properly, and the trachea becomes floppy and essentially collapses. It is not something he can grow out of. It is caused by his internal structure, which is not normal. Yes, over time his body can adapt, and he would be able to control his tracheomalacia better, but he would never just grow out of it. What we could do was be proactive and help open his lungs and trachea with daily breathing treatments (which take about ten minutes each time) combined with vest therapy. The vest therapy shakes his chest to help loosen the mucus, allowing for a better airway clearance. He also needed to start an oral steroid (given via the G-tube) to help with the inflammation in his lungs.

I cannot describe the kind of peace we had leaving her office that day. It was a peace like we had not experienced since Bracey's birth. In all of his six months of life, not a single other doctor had suggested breathing treatments to help open his airways. We were told over and over again he would grow out of the wheezing. For the first time in his life, I felt like Bracey was going to have an amazing future.

"Thank You, God, for Your daily mercies and for providing us with the perfect doctor for Bracey. Thank You for our doctor and her desire to heal little children."

Bracey's wheezing seemed to diminish overnight. We could no longer hear him breathing. This was so amazing. However, per our doctor's orders, we continued the breathing treatments every six hours and continued to see our speech therapist to help with the suck, swallow, breathe concept.

August 25, 2008—Six Months Old

With the wonderful new relief at Bracey's progress, Bracey saw his speech therapist again. She gave me lots of ideas of how to get Bracey to try to drink from a bottle. I went home that day completely stressed out. Was Bracey ready to try a bottle again? Was I ready for Bracey to try a bottle?

So many mixed emotions were running through my head. After praying and talking it over with Torrey and our doctor, we decided it was time to let Bracey try. He was almost seven months old, and he had not had any bottles since he was one month old. Would he even know what to do with it? I wondered.

His speech therapist recommended we go very slowly and explained Bracey would be picky since he hadn't had anything in his mouth in six months. We would need to try many different types of techniques before we would find the one Bracey could enjoy.

I had everything ready for Bracey just in case he stopped breathing. I had him hooked up to the oxygen monitor, I had the oxygen machine ready, I had the suction machine ready, and I had Torrey by my side. We took a deep breath and proceeded to give Bracey his bottle.

One swallow, two swallows, three swallows, four swallows, five swallows, and so it continued. His oxygen level remained at 100 percent. Before we knew it, Bracey drank three ounces of formula without even a single indication of distress. I gave him the last ounce and a half via his G-tube because he looked like he was getting tired. Then for dinner, he took his entire four and a half ounces by bottle, and right before bed, he fell asleep eating about another three ounces by bottle. Torrey and I were incredibly overwhelmed by Bracey. He was a champion!

I was very emotional the first couple times I fed him this way. I had forgotten what a tremendous feeling it was to actually get to feed my baby. To have him looking up at me while I provide his belly with yummy fullness and feeling that one-of-a-kind connection with my baby. It is the best feeling ever. I knew this was all God's doing. God allowed Bracey to take a bottle as if he had always had one. He allowed Torrey and I to experience a different kind of bond with him, one I had longed for since the day he was born.

The next day, Bracey took every single feed by bottle. The speech therapist could not believe it. She said she had never seen or heard of this happening so quickly. Bracey had not had a bottle in over six months. He should not have taken it so easily. Bracey took off with his bottle feedings like a champ. I knew in my heart he would no longer need that G-tube.

Months went by, and Bracey continued to grow and thrive. Our daily lives revolved around breathing treatments, doctor appointments, occupational and speech therapy, and just playing together. For the first time since Bracey's birth, I no longer feared for his life. As life moved on, Bracey hit fun milestones. He rolled over, he sat up, he army crawled, and he jabbered words. Due to all of his setbacks, his milestones were quite delayed; however, he still reached them. Things continued to progress.

October 2008—Eight Months Old

I hadn't been feeling well for a few days. It was midmorning, and I was having severe vertigo-like symptoms. My sister was downstairs that morning. All I could do was text her and ask her for help. I couldn't care for Bracey. I felt so sick. I literally had to crawl on my hands and knees to get back to my bedroom. I had never been that sick. The next morning, I was feeling better but had a lingering headache. My sister suggested I might be pregnant. I chuckled and said, "Yeah right." Having another baby was nowhere on my radar. She bought me a pregnancy test just in case. I figured it was a waste of money, but I took the test just for her. Oh! My! Word! I could not believe it. Tears instantly filled my eyes. Tears of joy and fear.

How would I give Torrey the news? How would he handle it? I was overwhelmed with fear. Bracey was still fragile. His needs were great. What if this baby had special needs as well? How would we emotionally, physically, and financially handle two special-needs children? Fears of doubt and uncertainty clouded what should have been an exciting time in our lives. I knew it was God's timing even though it wasn't in mine. When I told Torrey, he was shocked but surprisingly excited for our new adventure. He hugged me and said, "We're in this together."

I went in to see a doctor right away. The doctor referred me to a high-risk doctor to follow me through this pregnancy. I appreciated the thoroughness of the exams of me and the baby. On top of the typical pregnancy ultrasounds and blood work, I had a fetal echocardiogram and a comprehensive assessment of the fetal anatomy. We hoped to be as prepared as possible for this precious baby.

January 2009—Almost One Year Old

Bracey had been doing well for a few months. We continued seeing his lung specialist and speech therapist regularly. Torrey and I felt it was time to address Bracey's hands. Bracey was born without thumbs or radius bones on either hand. His hands were severely curved in. We were finally given the all clear from his pulmonologist and were ready to take the next step in helping Bracey be the best he could be.

We met with a pediatric hand specialist in Indianapolis. He was quite familiar with radial dysplasia and had great outcomes with his patients. We met with this hand specialist a few different times, and we felt comfortable with the procedure recommended. Of course, we were still nervous. The surgery would entail straightening his ulna (centralization of the ulna) and turning one of his fingers into a thumb (pollicization). We went through the emotions I think any parent would go through. We questioned ourselves. *Are we doing the right thing for Bracey?* This was basically an elective surgery. Bracey did not need these surgeries to survive. Yes, he would be physically able to do more things if he had these surgeries, but they weren't required. While we had definitely made strides in the right direction with Bracey's tracheomalacia, he was still a medically challenging little boy.

After hours of praying, speaking with all of his doctors, and speaking with family and close friends, Torrey and I ultimately made the decision to go ahead with his reconstructive hand surgery. The doctor would perform an external fixation and distraction osteogenisis and centralization for radius dysplasia. Basically, the doctor would straighten his hands and lengthen his ulnas (the outer bone of the forearm), using an external fixation device. The extensive reconstruction would require a series of surgeries.

February 19, 2009—One Year Old

Bracey endured his first round of hand surgeries. Although we were nervous about this, we had peace from God this was the right thing to do for Bracey. During the surgery, his pulmonologist and his GI doctor were both with him, and they did two scopes. One looked at his esophagus, and one explored his trachea and lungs. Then they both came out and spoke with us about the scopes. Bracey had a very swollen esophagus, and it was covered with candida (a fungal infection most likely due to his breathing treatments) and large signs of acid reflux. The doctor was amazed Bracey had not shown signs of pain from the acid reflux. His tracheomalacia was even more severe than the doctor had expected. She explained the possibilities of a tracheotomy. These findings caught us completely off guard. Bracey was mainly there to have his hands corrected, and we were given this huge amount of difficult information.

"What does all of this mean?" I asked. Basically, Bracey was an amazing little boy with a high pain tolerance. His body was adapting to what it needed to do for him to function. He needed to be put on medication for the acid reflux and for the swelling in his esophagus. He would remain on breathing treatments every four hours. The doctors went on and told us that, for Bracey, even though he looked like he was doing well and all was healthy on the outside, his insides were very weak. Bracey was a fighter and didn't complain much, so we didn't know when his insides needed help. All we could do was provide the medication he needed to continue to fight his tracheomalacia.

A couple of hours later, the hand surgeon came out and declared Bracey was doing well. He had needed to be intubated due to his breathing, but he was doing fine. The doctor was able to do the straightening of his hands, but he was unable to do the lengthening of the arm bone. Bracey's hands were tighter than the doctor had anticipated. He was unable to stretch them as much as he would have liked to. It was just too much for Bracey to handle. They were, however, much straighter than before.

Bracey did well that night with his recovery. We were even able to take him home the next afternoon. He didn't show any signs of pain, and Bracey was so happy. We were surprised and relieved he was doing so well.

It was too good to last. Around midnight that evening, Bracey started crying, and we could not calm him down. Bracey very rarely cried. We figured his hands were hurting, so we gave him some pain medicine and hoped he would calm down soon. He continued to cry and not just a fussy whine but a full-blown screaming cry. I had never heard him cry this hard.

He was beginning to make his wheezing sounds I hadn't heard in months. I knew we needed to calm him down. The only thing that seemed to help was pushing him all around the house in his stroller. He would fall asleep for twenty minutes, but then he would start screaming all over again. More pushing would help him fall asleep but never for long. This went on all night. Torrey would take a couple of hours of pushing him around in the stroller, and then I would take a turn.

Around five in the morning, we called the on-call hand doctor, and she said he was most likely in some pain because the numbing medication had worn off. We were advised if he continued it throughout the day, we should bring Bracey back to the hospital to be checked out. Well, he continued it for more than twelve more hours, and we decided he needed to go back to the hospital. Something wasn't right.

On Sunday morning, we were back in the hospital. The doctors put Bracey on morphine and fentanyl, but still Bracey remained in pain and agony. His hand doctor assured us his hands were fine and they were not the cause of this immense pain.

His GI doctor and pulmonologist both came in and said he could be in pain from the scraping of his esophagus that they did to get tissue samples, the swelling of his esophagus, and the irritation left behind from being intubated while in surgery. All of these combined could and probably were causing him great pain. However, since the pain meds were not working, and they could not visually see the cause for the pain, they wanted to take Bracey back into surgery to do another bronchoscopy and endoscopy.

I was reluctant for them to take Bracey back into surgery. If his pain was due to his already swollen esophagus, then why would they want to go back down it again? However, I was not thinking clearly, and I just couldn't stand to see Bracey in any more pain, so they took him back.

Tears were streaming down my face. My heart was aching for Bracey. What was going on inside his body? What had happened? Bracey had seemed to be doing so well.

The doctors reported that Bracey's esophagus was basically swollen shut from the throat down. They administered large doses of steroids to help with the swelling and said Bracey had also caught a virus that was attacking his lungs and causing a great amount of mucus. They were able to suction a lot of his mucus out in surgery, but his body was still producing large amounts of it as he fought the virus.

Things went from bad to worse within the hour. Bracey was finally resting, and my parents had just left to go home after a long, intense day. Torrey and I were sitting next to Bracey, and I could hear him wheezing. Almost immediately after I heard the wheezing, he became restless, and his monitor started going off. His oxygen levels were declining. I could tell he needed to be suctioned out. Torrey called for a nurse to come and check on him, and everything moved very quickly.

I shouted, "He needs suctioned out!" The nurse was scrambling for the suction bowl, as it was not set up or attached to the wall. Bracey's oxygen level dropped to 40 percent, and he was unresponsive within seconds. I was yelling for other nurses, and quickly, a team of doctors and nurses were surrounding my baby. Torrey and I stepped out of the way to let the doctors work on him. Minutes passed, and no one was talking to us or telling us what was going on.

As Torrey and I stood outside Bracey's room, the hospital chaplain came up and asked to pray with us. With tears streaming down our faces, we prayed with the chaplain while I never took my eyes off Bracey's room. The chaplain stayed with us for quite some time.

After just over thirty minutes of working with Bracey, they were able to stabilize him enough to be placed in the PICU. Because Bracey's throat was so swollen, they could not intubate him through his mouth, so they had to put in a nasotracheal intubation. They had to suction him every hour to keep up with the amount of mucus his body was producing. The suctioning was terrible. It was tough to hold down my precious little boy while they suctioned him out. The tube went up his nose and down into his trachea.

He spent eleven days in the PICU. Those eleven days were filled with ups and downs. Only one parent was allowed to sleep in the PICU. It was tough telling Torrey goodnight every evening, but I couldn't pull myself away from my baby. The nurses quickly believed me that when Bracey's oxygen level started to decline, his oxygen would not come back up without intervention such as suctioning. Bracey was not coughing on his own to help the secretions come out. I would pat his back every so often to try to make him cough.

The child life specialists would come around and bring Bracey things to try to help raise his spirits, but Bracey was not interested. Our next few days became a routine. Every twenty minutes or so, Bracey's monitor would beep, and I would see his oxygen dropping. I would run out into the hall to get a nurse and then have to hold my little guy down while they suctioned him out. I was mentally, physically, and spiritually exhausted.

Our friends and family tried to encourage us. I constantly heard the perfect Christian cliché. "He will be okay. He is in God's hands. God will take care of him." As a Christian, I know these things, and I believe these things, but right then, I was hurting so badly. I felt as if God wasn't hearing my prayers—and certainly wasn't answering them the way I felt they should be answered. What was He trying to teach me? Why was He using *my* helpless baby to teach me something? Use *me*! Torture *me*! Make *me* go through these painful procedures. As tough as it was, I continued to trust in God, and I reminded myself Bracey was in His hands.

Bracey had made a full recovery by the first of April. He still had his external fixators attached to his arms, which were annoying to him.

Our weeks and months were filled with numerous doctors' appointments and therapies. From the beginning, we knew Bracey's life would consist of doctors, hospitals, and therapies. As the weeks and months went by, I continued to work with Bracey as he struggled reaching milestones, such as eating solid foods, walking, feeding himself, independent sleeping, and so on. Bracey was my whole world. At that point, I wouldn't have had it any other way.

July 2009—Seventeen Months Old

Summer was in full swing as we anxiously awaited the arrival of our baby girl. On July 25, Bracey became a big brother. It was such an exciting time in our lives. Our beautiful and healthy daughter, Brynn, was an amazing gift to our family. Bracey, now seventeen months old, was still not walking or eating solid foods. We knew he was delayed by all of his physical trials, so we were not concerned about him walking yet. He was starting to cruise along furniture and trying to take steps, so he was moving in the right direction.

Bracey's doctors and I were much more concerned about his inability to eat solid foods without choking on them. His pulmonologist and GI doctor both decided to do yet another scope to see if Bracey's esophagus needed to be dilated or was developing another TEF (tear in his esophagus).

The scopes came back showing that Bracey's peristalsis muscles in his digestive tract were not working. Peristalsis is when muscles contract to help push foods down into the stomach. Basically, Bracey would swallow a solid food, and it would just sit there, because the muscles were not contracting to move the food down. The doctors hoped that with time, and as Bracey grew, his muscles would mature and start working properly.

October 2009—Twenty Months Old

Bracey had developed a respiratory infection—a cold. But with Bracey, colds are never *just* colds. His colds usually resulted in him going to the hospital. That October was rough. Once again, Bracey ended up in the hospital with a respiratory infection. This was becoming our way of life. Unfortunately, we were beginning to know this routine all too well. We knew simply going to the ER for medication was not going to help. The doctors would take one x-ray of Bracey's lungs and ship us off to the pediatric ward. So, before we even left for the ER, I had our bags packed, ready to be admitted.

This time, it was much harder for me because I had to be away from my three-month-old baby girl. I was torn in two directions. I longed so badly to be cuddling Brynn, and I missed her so much that my heart hurt. But I knew where I needed to be, and God gave me peace. Torrey brought her to see me, and I spent time with her at the hospital.

Bracey recovered well enough to go home within four days. We were down to breathing treatments every four hours instead of every two. We were instructed to finish out his steroids and monitor his oxygen levels.

What is God continually trying to teach me? Why did He give me a beautiful baby boy, only to watch him endure pain and struggles for, quite possibly, the rest of his life? Living in hospital rooms, having surgery after surgery, fighting to eat, fighting to breathe, fighting to sit up, and fighting to walk … fighting for his life! We had packed up our entire lives and moved in with my parents for the added help and support. We left our jobs, our home, our church, and our friends.

"God, please help me understand! I continue to search for answers from You, Lord. I don't want to do this anymore. I don't want Bracey to go through any more trials. I don't want Bracey to have to endure any more pain or struggles. Heavenly Father, I'm not sure what You're doing or why You're doing this, but I know You are breaking my heart. You're breaking my pride, my self-dependence, and You're helping me to love by faith, and I surrender Bracey completely to You. Please use him for Your purpose. Please give me the peace that we are right where You want us to be. I want what You want in my life. Your plan is better than mine, and I embrace the change You are working in me. I love You, Lord. Amen."

Seven more weeks went by, and Bracey was doing great. We were still working toward trying to eat solids without choking, but he wasn't ready. So, we were still mainly doing bottle feedings and baby foods.

December 2009—Twenty-Two Months Old

Christmas was upon us. Everyone was in the Christmas spirit. Everyone except for our little buddy, Bracey. He was starting to get sick again. I called his pulmonologist at the onset of his first junky cough. Bracey's coughs were very distinctive. His coughs were always shockingly loud and bronchial sounding, even when his coughs were triggered by a laugh. We had learned that proactive, aggressive action was the key to maintaining Bracey's health. His doctor called in a steroid for him, and we upped his daily breathing treatments to four times a day. After twenty-four hours of being on the steroid, we thought, *Wow, are we going to get away without him having to be hospitalized?* He seemed to be improving.

We decided to keep our plans to visit family, as he really seemed to be better. The first night away, Bracey went downhill quickly. We were disappointed, but we knew he needed to get back to see his doctor.

We packed everything back up the morning of December

22 and headed home. Of course, our family understood and supported us, like they've always done. It just seemed tougher than usual, lonelier. Knowing your entire family is in one place and you can't be there is lonely. We tried to focus on being thankful for the few hours we did get to spend with them.

We called the on-call pulmonologist, and Bracey was admitted into the hospital yet again. This stay occurred during flu season, so the hospital would not allow Brynn to come and visit in Bracey's room. This was heartbreaking for me. The doctor thought maybe Bracey would only need a couple days of aggressive treatment and then could go home for Christmas.

Bracey fought hard. He slept a lot those couple of days. I was in constant prayer that God would allow us to be home for Christmas. While the hospital was our second home, and we loved our nurses and doctors, we wanted to be home for Christmas. Bracey had to be able to sleep through the night without desatting (lowering of oxygen levels) before they would allow us to go home.

The morning of December 24, I was so excited because I had been watching his monitor all night, and I knew he would be going home. He wasn't back to his baseline of two breathing treatments a day, but he was well enough to enjoy Christmas at home.

We packed up our things, and on Christmas Eve, we went home. We got to celebrate our first Christmas as a family of four. Bracey was sleepy most of the day, but we were all together for Christmas.

Bracey made a full recovery from that bout of pneumonia. It always took him a couple weeks to get back to his baseline of two breathing treatments a day, but we made it. Bracey is certainly a fighter. At almost two years old, he was working hard at walking and talking. He loved music and dancing. He was still not taking any solids, but we worked on it daily, little by little. I just knew that one of these days, he would take off and start eating everything in sight.

January 21, 2010—Almost Two Years Old

Ever since I gave Bracey completely over to God (which was months after his birth), I've had peace regarding Bracey. My daily outlook changed. The way I reacted to Bracey's health changed. I stayed relatively calm during stressful events in his life. I was at peace knowing that he was God's child. I am to love him, nurture him, and protect him the best I can. Ultimately, though, he belongs to God. I had peace knowing Bracey's heavenly Father was his ultimate protector, and although God doesn't promise that nothing bad will ever happen, He does promise to be with us during those bad times.

That one evening, January 21, I momentarily lost sight of those truths. It was a normal evening. Bedtime routine was normal. Bracey was back to his baseline of healthy. *Everything was normal.* Bracey went to bed around eight o'clock, as usual, and without any signs of being sick.

After about an hour, we heard a screech through his baby monitor. I went in to check on him. It was dark in his room, but the hallway light was streaming in, and I could tell he was on his back convulsing. I screamed for Torrey and flipped on the lights. Torrey ran in and picked him up immediately as he continued to convulse. We called out Bracey's name but received no response, just continued convulsions.

I was in a major state of panic. Bracey's eyes were completely rolled back in his head, and he was foaming at the mouth. We could not tell if he was breathing at this point. I called 911. My parents ran upstairs because they heard the commotion. My emotions overtook my ability to think clearly and calmly. As Torrey was working with Bracey, I grabbed my phone and called my mother-in-law, Cathy. I was breathing heavily and fast. I needed someone to calm me down. I explained to her something was wrong with Bracey. He wasn't responding and was shaking out of control. Over and over again, Cathy told me to calm down and take a deep breath. She asked where Torrey was, but I couldn't answer her. I couldn't talk. I was only sobbing. In that moment, I had lost complete control of myself. I soon heard my mom yelling for me, notifying me the ambulance was here, and I abruptly hung up with Cathy.

I watched as a police officer took Bracey out of Torrey's hands and ran him to the paramedics. Bracey was still shaking and unresponsive. The paramedics said he was having a seizure.

From the time we found Bracey until he stopped convulsing was about fifteen minutes. He was still unresponsive and remained unresponsive for over an hour after the convulsions stopped. At the local emergency room, the doctor was very friendly. Bracey woke up and was responding, so the doctor dismissed him and chalked it up to a grand febrile seizure (a seizure that occurs when you rapidly spike a high fever). The doctor did not see the need to do any tests, or anything for that matter. He told us to follow up with Bracey's pediatrician and was discharging us. Well, this mama came unglued!

Did I mention how calm, cool, and collected I had been for almost two years? Well, that night I snapped. I was sick of ER doctors dismissing Bracey just because they had no clue what was wrong with him. They took one look at him and, in my opinion, got scared. They had never heard of VACTERL, so when they saw his numbers look good and he looked good, they sent us on our way. I had had enough of that.

There I was, sitting in a hospital bed, cuddling my baby who just had a prolonged seizure event that left him unable to wake up for over an hour! And the doctor just told me to go home. I don't think so! I remember so clearly my conversation with that doctor that night.

"Do you have children, Doctor?"

"Yes," he said.

"Okay, can you pretend for a minute you are not a doctor and you are a nonmedical parent? You just walked into your baby's room, and you saw your son convulsing, eyes rolled back into his head, foaming at the mouth, and nonresponsive. On top of that, he is a special-needs child who, up to this point in his life, hasn't had any mental disabilities. Imagine that your child has spent the majority of his life, of almost two years, in and out of the hospital. He has had hundreds of tests, x-rays, surgeries, ER visits, doctor appointments, and therapies—along with medical students wanting to study him, being poked and prodded. He's been through sleepless nights of just trying to breathe, having to eat through a G-tube, having to fight for his life multiple times. You have had to physically resuscitate him more than once. And now you rush to the emergency room because you don't know or understand what is happening to your baby. For all you know, he is dying. Despite all you've been through with your child, you had never experienced seizures before. Then you get to the emergency room, and you have a friendly doctor who just dismisses the entire event. As if it's normal. He tells you to just follow up with your pediatrician. What would you do? How would you react?"

The doctor stood there, tears in his eyes, and looked at me and gently said, "I am sorry." I told him I was sorry I just unloaded all of that on him. My emotions got the best of me. I was scared.

He assured me he completely understood what it must feel like to be told your child is fine and to go home after having such an episode. But as an ER doctor, it was his responsibility to get his patients back to a stable condition, and that was exactly what he did. Bracey was stable and was showing no signs of trouble. In the doctor's eyes, Bracey was safe to go home and follow up with his pediatrician.

I told him I understood, and while I did understand his rationalization, I didn't understand it. What if a seizure happened again tonight? What if the next one was bigger or longer? I just didn't understand. I was not okay with it, but we took our discharge papers, along with the doctor's notes, and headed home. That night, I didn't sleep at all. Bracey slept right beside me.

I prayed most of the night, searching out God's truths.

"Again, Lord, why did this happen? What, if anything, are You trying to teach me? Were You wanting to see if I would fail at trusting You? In the scariest moments, yes, Lord, I did not give it to You. I panicked. I freaked out. I allowed my emotions to take over. I yelled, I cried, I, in that moment, did not rely on You. I feared the worst was happening. I feared I was going to lose my son. The baby I had fought so hard for. The baby I tried so hard to protect and love. The baby I fought to get the best care possible for within our means. In that moment, I was a hysterical mess. I was the person I never wanted to be! Please, God, never allow my emotions to take me to that dark place again. No matter what You have for us as a family, Lord, please do not let me allow my emotions to turn me into someone I'm not."

The next morning, we were able to get an appointment with Bracey's amazing pediatrician. He got us in right away.

He explained the type of seizure Bracey had and helped me to understand. However, to be cautious, he ordered an EEG. An EEG would help rule out any brain disorders.

January 27, 2010—Almost Two Years Old

We took Bracey to his hospital in Indy where he had an EEG. He had had one as an infant, but due to Bracey's brain anatomy and his most recent seizure, the doctor felt this test needed to be done again to make sure nothing significant was going on. It came back normal.

The next few months were great for Bracey. Our days were filled with doctor appointments and therapies. Also, during these months, Bracey began to really walk, talk, and develop quite a personality. He always wanted to make others laugh. He was a typical little boy who got into everything. He was faster than me at times. I can't even begin to count how many times I found miscellaneous items in the toilet, in his crib, in Brynn's crib, or in the dog's food dish. This little guy kept me on my toes.

March 2010—Two Years Old

In late March, Torrey received a job offer to be an assistant athletic director and coach at a Christian school, which moved us back to Northwest Indiana. We were excited about the job and being back near our friends and other family.

It was tough leaving my family; however, we knew it was time to move on. Bracey was stronger and was growing, and this was a great opportunity for our little family. Another tough aspect of moving was having to lose our amazing pediatrician. However, I knew we would keep our specialists in Indy, which gave me great peace. We were only going to be two hours away from them, and that was doable. Everything fell into place. God provided a job and a home for us all in the same week. The doors were opened for us, and we walked right through!

May 2010—Two Years Old

The next few months were filled with adjustments—adjusting to a new home, a new job, a new city, a new church, new friends, new doctors, new therapists, and so on. Our lives quickly got busy. Torrey began working right away with his new school. He was beginning soccer practices and doing summer maintenance for the school. I was busy chasing after two little ones and enjoying the beautiful summer in our new home. Life was great!

Being a mother of two toddlers was interesting, to say the least. Although certainly a complicated child as far as health goes, Bracey was completely normal as far as toddler trouble. One afternoon that summer, I left an open box of goldfish crackers on the ottoman while I quickly ran to the restroom. I wasn't gone more than about sixty seconds, but when I came back to the living room, that box was half-empty, and my children were playing in a giant pile of goldfish!

Later that week, I had to go grocery shopping. Shopping with two toddlers can only be described as dreadful. Unfortunately, the store at that time only had single child seat carts, requiring one child to sit in the basket part of the cart, with the food. I was already tired when we started and just wanted to get in, get my things, and get out. That was wishful thinking. I was looking at my list, getting the things I needed, all the while telling the kids to sit down, use your inside voices, stop touching each other, and so on. I could not make it to the cracker aisle fast enough—the blessed aisle where I grabbed a box of crackers and prayed they would occupy the children long enough to finish my shopping. I was moving right along after that, having a happy moment, when I realized the crackers must be working because my kids had been very quiet. Suddenly, I slipped and found myself flat on my butt in the middle of the aisle. After the initial shock, I stood up and realized there was orange yogurt all over my pants. Bracey kept saying, "Uh oh, Mommy okay?" I was a bit annoyed someone would spill something and just leave it there. I found a worker and told him about the spill someone had left and how I had fallen in it. I'm sure he could sense my annoyance. He gave me some paper towels and headed off to clean the aisle. I wiped my pants and went on my way, still frustrated about the whole thing. Seriously, who would spill stuff and leave it there without telling someone? It was just rude!

Seconds later, my brain processed that Bracey was still saying, "Uh oh." I finally acknowledged him, and when I did, I realized he had orange yogurt all over him and in the cart. *What?* It was *my* son who had opened a tub of yogurt and spilled it all over the floor. I could not get out of that store fast enough!

Bracey had a fabulous summer. We continued his daily treatments to manage his tracheomalacia and his poor motility in his esophagus and stomach. Things were going well for our family. We were well into the soccer and school year season. We had joined a church and were getting involved there. Bracey was healthy, for Bracey. We felt settled in our new lives in northern Indiana.

October 2010—Two and a Half Years Old

Fall of 2010 had officially arrived. Bracey had another fantastic few months. The longer we lived with Bracey, the more we learned about his tricky body. We knew his triggers, his early signs of getting sick, his good seasons, and his bad seasons. We knew Bracey had gone quite a while without getting sick, and we needed to get prepared for his inevitable fall sickness. And in late October 2010, Bracey did just that. He got sick ... really sick.

October 27, 2010—Two and a Half Years

Bracey and Brynn went down for their regular nap. Bracey had been acting perfectly healthy. After their two-and-a-half-hour nap, I knew immediately Bracey was sick. Bracey was notorious for going to sleep feeling fine and acting normal and waking up with a raging fever, cough, low oxygen levels, and difficulty breathing. I knew right away this onset of infection needed medical attention before he got worse.

We lined up care for Brynn and headed off to the ER. We were very fortunate to have my sister-in-law, Amanda, and brother-in-law, Tom, living so close by. Brynn loved spending time with them, and I never had to worry about her, although I deeply missed her when I had to be away.

The ER was busy that night, and I knew this was going to be a long evening. Torrey carried Bracey in, and I signed paperwork. I told the receptionist he had a high fever and his oxygen levels were lower than they should be. She got Bracey registered, and we began the waiting game.

After thirty-five minutes of anxiously waiting, I knew Bracey needed attention. His color was turning a bit ashy, and his fever was up. Torrey and I were getting nervous and agitated. I knew Bracey was headed down a dangerous road and needed immediate help (after all, we were at the ER). Torrey went to speak with the front desk and demand they see Bracey now. He signaled for me to come over, and I picked up my helpless child and headed straight back into the ER.

We were put in a room, and they checked his fever and oxygen. His fever was up to 103.4, and his oxygen level was at 83 percent. We had seen this before and knew how quickly things could go south for Bracey. They gave him medicine to reduce his fever and started him on oxygen right away. They ordered x-rays and breathing treatments. We gave them our pulmonologist's name and number and requested she be called. She would be able to instruct the ER doctors on what needed to be done.

Bracey was not considered stable at that point. They brought the x-ray technicians to his room. The doctor came back in shortly after the x-rays and said 57 percent of his lungs were filled with pneumonia. I was astounded he could have so much infection in his lungs and we hadn't seen any signs of it. He literally fell asleep healthy and woke up very sick. We knew this was how Bracey's body worked.

Bracey's pulmonologist wanted Bracey transported to Indy, a

two-hour drive, so she could treat him. I, of course, knew Bracey needed to be in Indy, but my heart was breaking to leave Brynn behind, not knowing how long I would have to be apart from her.

After fifteen hours in the ER, Bracey was still on 100 percent oxygen, and he still had a fever and nasty cough, but we were ready to be transported down to Indy. I rode with Bracey in the transport ambulance. I had never made it to Indy so quickly before!

As sad as I was to be away from Brynn, I was so relieved to be down in Indy. I knew we would get excellent care with the doctors and nurses who knew him best. I cannot express the immense peace I had just knowing we were at Bracey's hospital. The doctors and nurses there are fantastic.

Bracey stayed the same for the next forty-eight hours. While he was not getting any worse, he was also not getting any better. He had an IV in his foot, which he hated. He had been doing breathing treatments every two hours for more than two days. He was so tired. It seemed like by the time a treatment was done and he was just about to fall asleep, the therapist was coming in again for his next round of treatments. He had zero appetite and was very weak. Two more days went by, and he was finally sitting up and much more alert. His treatments had been decreased to every four hours.

On day four, he was able to come off of the oxygen and was cleared to take short wagon rides around the hospital floor. He loved doing this! He was still quite weak, but he was improving.

His sister, Brynn, got to come on day four to see him, and that made me very happy. It is heartbreaking as a mom to have to be apart from your babies, no matter what the circumstances. I was so thankful my parents brought her to see us. When they walked into the room with Brynn, Bracey's face lit up. He was so ecstatic to see them all, as was I. There was always a calming peace when family/friends came to visit us at the hospital. Being surrounded by family with laughter, real food, and hugs brings this incredible, calming peace to me. There is a great deal to be said for just knowing we were not alone.

Bracey continued to do better and better, and the doctors agreed to take the IV out. This was a huge turning point for Bracey. Every time Bracey needed an IV in his foot, he hated it so much more than in his arms. He refused to walk while the IV was in. The minute they removed the IV, Bracey excelled in his recovery. He was able to walk. Although still weak, we took walks, and he got a nice warm bath. He could just sit in the tub and play with a couple of toys. How soothing and refreshing that bathtub was for him. That evening, Bracey was like a new kid. He was talking, laughing, playing, and eating again. He was playing and responding with the therapists who came in. My little guy was coming back to me!

On day six, we were able to take Bracey home and continue his healing process there. Breathing treatments continued around the clock, every four hours, until the coughing was completely gone. He had to continue all his medications until they were gone as well, but we got to go home! After six long, sleepless, emotional days, we were a family again.

With each and every sickness that comes Bracey's way, I learn a little bit more about how his body works. Bracey's organs and bones are developed differently than most, which makes things interesting when trying to figure him out. Hospital life was tough on our family, and I was determined to keep him out of the hospital as much as possible. More than ever, I studied him. I watched and listened intently to his body signals. I monitored his sleeping, eating, playing, and breathing patterns. I became obsessed with Bracey. I would go into his room at night and lie next to him just to listen to him breathing. I would lie there with my hand on his chest for hours.

I have always checked on my kids while they are sleeping. Before I fell asleep, every night, I went into their rooms while they were sleeping. I prayed over them, kissed them, and adjusted their covers. This, I believe, is a typical parenting thing. But my obsession with my son was atypical.

For weeks after our discharge from the hospital, I didn't leave Bracey. This kind of obsession was very unhealthy for me *and* him. I was physically and emotionally exhausted. Why was I doing this? What had changed? I realized I had become weak in my reliance on God's plan for my son and allowed terrible thoughts to come into my head. Thoughts of the unknown. Thoughts of the what ifs. I had given Bracey completely to God a few months after his birth. Why was I questioning Him now? I had to let go of those unknowns and what ifs. Allowing those things to overtake my life was a scary place to live. I did not want to continue to live there. I was still determined to keep Bracey out of the hospital as much as possible but in a more realistic way.

Bracey was going to get sick again—and again. It is how Bracey's body works. His body doesn't fight off germs and viruses like mine. I decided to become more proactive about it. There must be some sign he was getting sick. Something, no matter how small it was, had to be an indication that he was getting sick. And on December 6, 2010, I noticed that sign.

December 6, 2010—Almost Three Years Old

We had only been home from the hospital for five weeks before I noticed the sign that Bracey was getting sick. The morning of December 6 was like any other morning. The kids were playing in the family room while their favorite television show, *The Backyardigans*, was on. I was in the kitchen making breakfast. I sat my children in their high chairs and gave them their scrambled eggs with cheese, one of our favorites. We were eating and talking/jabbering, and I heard a cough. I handed Bracey his sippy cup to take a drink. Remember, Bracey had poor motility, so, while he was eating solids now, food would often get stuck in his throat, and he had to take drinks to help it get down. However, the cough triggered my motherly instincts to pay closer attention to him during his breakfast. As Brynn was shoveling the food down her throat, Bracey coughed again. I give him his sippy cup again, and he took a drink, but the drink came back up right away. His food was certainly stuck, and the drink wasn't helping him. My insides were freaking out, but I knew I needed to remain calm for Bracey. I calmly yet swiftly got him from his chair. I could see the fear in his eyes, as his food wasn't going down and was blocking his airway.

He had a floppy trachea (tracheomalacia), and coughing, sneezing, laughing, and swallowing could all make his trachea close momentarily. This time, the food wasn't going to go down. I had to get it out. I looked into my son's terrified eyes and smiled and reassured him it would be okay. I told him to remain calm and the food would come up. I told him I was going to hug him and squeeze him. I quickly yet calmly hugged him from the back while squeezing, and after the second squeeze, his food came out. I gave him a drink and a tight hug and kiss. He didn't want any more food, and Brynn was finished, so I put them both back in the family room to watch their show.

I quietly went to my room, shut the door, and cried my eyes out. I thanked God for giving me the strength and sound mind to help my child even though I was freaking out on the inside. That morning went on, but Bracey seemed a bit off.

I called his pulmonologist to tell her of the morning's events. Being the amazing, loving, and most proactive doctor I had ever known, she started Bracey on steroids right away. She said it sounded like he could be getting an infection. She wanted to head it off if possible. So, before naptime, I headed to our local pharmacy and picked up his prescriptions. Bracey took one dose of his Orapred (steroid) and a breathing treatment and then was off for naptime.

His nap was much longer than usual. He woke up after four hours, and he only roused then because of his cough. I knew he was getting sick. I went into his room to get him, and he was burning up. I took his temperature, not surprised it was 101.2. I called the on-call doctor, as it was now after-hours Indy. Indy is a one-hour time zone away. The on-call doctor started him on an antibiotic and increased his breathing treatments to every four hours instead of twice a day.

With proactive treatments and around-the-clock breathing treatments, we were able to keep Bracey out of the hospital during that infection. This was the very first time Bracey had been sick that we were able to manage it from home. I strongly believe that being assertive and proactive with his treatments, along with my attention to early signs and symptoms, allowed us to catch the infection before it worsened to the point of needing hospitalization. What a great feeling it was to think maybe we would be able to catch his early signs next time!

I thanked God for helping me stay alert and for showing me Bracey's signs. I thanked his doctor for her love, care, and being proactive in Bracey's health management.

The holidays came and went quickly, as they usually do if you're not in a hospital. It is such a special time to celebrate with family and friends. We were able to break away from the routine of everyday life and simply enjoy being together, celebrating what God had given us. And, as always, January came, and life returned to routine. January always seems to be a more somber month than others. Its bitter cold winds, snow, ice, and the fact it's dark before dinner time make it such a gloomy month. Our routine was back in full swing. Torrey was coaching, and I was home, tending to two beautiful babies. Life was moving along, well, at least until January 27, 2011.

January 27, 2011—Almost Three Years Old

I noticed Bracey was acting tired and not interested in eating. I was puttering around, cleaning the house, and when I checked on him, Bracey had fallen asleep on the couch. I leaned over, listening, and heard a slight rumble in his chest. He felt hot to the touch. In my experience with Bracey, the rumbling in his chest meant infection had already set in and he needed medical attention. I called his pulmonologist, and she encouraged me to bring him down to Indy to the ER. Her office would be closed by the time I got to Indy, but she said she would meet me at the children's hospital emergency room. So, I packed Bracey up, and down we went.

By the time we got down to Indy, Bracey had developed a

cough. It was very tight sounding and seemed like it was painful to him. I was so relieved when I walked into that ER and saw our favorite doctor waiting for us.

The nurse took his vitals, and his oxygen was at 91 percent. He had a slight fever of 100.0. His doctor ordered an x-ray. It came back showing slight infection in his left lung. She and I discussed the possibilities of admitting him. Winter is a terrible time to be hospitalized because there is a lot of sickness/germs going around in January. And if Bracey caught anything extra while there, it could send him to the PICU.

After talking with her, we decided I could take Bracey home. He needed to be on steroids, antibiotics, and breathing treatments around the clock, and he would have his oximeter machine connected to him at all times. If his oxygen dropped below 90 percent for a continuous amount of time, he would need to be admitted to be placed on oxygen. After a long day in Indy, we drove home that evening. Torrey and I would take shifts throughout the night to administer his treatments. We had long nights and days, but once again, we were able to manage this infection from home, and healing at home is way better than healing in a hospital.

Bracey had a rough winter and spring in the year of 2011. He had a respiratory infection every six to eight weeks. Each infection lasted about two weeks, but he *never* had to be hospitalized. Although it was an extremely exhausting time of monitoring and treatments, it was totally worth it, for Bracey was able to heal from home!

Summer 2011—Three Years Old

I was ecstatic to welcome summer. Summertime months are Bracey's best time health-wise, and he was doing great! We decided it was time to start talking about continuing his hand reconstructive surgery. Torrey and I met with many doctors during the spring and early summer that year. We had a few critics who could not understand why we planned to put Bracey through the pain of an elective surgery. "Just let Bracey be and develop his own way," they would say.

It was absolutely one of the toughest decisions we made as parents. There was no part of me that wanted Bracey to endure surgery again. Torrey and I went back and forth for weeks. We listened to doctors and researched extensively, examining all the angles.

Was this an elective surgery? Yes, it was. Would this surgery greatly benefit and add value to Bracey's future? Absolutely, it would. His orthopedic doctor was very frank with us. He said we could wait until Bracey was older, but the older he was, the more complications could arise. It would be tougher for Bracey to adapt to his new hands. Bracey was three. He already used his hands adaptively, figuring out his own modified ways of doing things. Bracey would pick up food by sliding it with his pinky to his palm and then placing it in his mouth, he would also play with his toys in the same manner. His other fingers were stiff and did not extend. He primarily used his pinkies. This surgery could enhance his adaptation and make things much easier for him.

Due to the lengthy procedure and tough recovery, the doctor was only comfortable with doing one arm and hand at a time. I was terrified of putting Bracey through more surgery, but I knew his future would be better because of it. We were going to be able to give Bracey more use of his hands.

Without this surgery, Bracey would have to rely on adaptable tools for the rest of his life just to perform simple everyday tasks.

Bracey had severe congenital radial longitudinal deficiency. He was missing radius bones and thumbs in each arm and hand, which formed very short forearms and tiny hands that curled around his arms.

I imagine every parent wants the best for their child. I wanted the best for Bracey. If Torrey and I had the opportunity to give him that, why wouldn't we? So, on July 18, 2011, we gave him that opportunity. Bracey was to have a distraction osteogenesis (lengthening of forearms) and pollicization (creating thumbs from existing fingers). We gave Bracey the opportunity to add value and independency to his life.

July 18, 2011—Three Years Old

The day of surgery was upon us. It was a bittersweet day for me. I knew we were doing the right thing, but that doesn't mean it was easy. Old familiar feelings swiftly came back as I checked my baby into the pre-op that morning—heavy feelings of anxiety, sadness, fear, and anticipation for his new arms/hands.

We waited in that pre-op room for hours, as surgery was pushed back a couple hours. We tried to keep Bracey happy. We took him on small walks down the hall and played games with him, but how do you keep a starving three-year-old happy? As he was growing more agitated, I prayed God would calm his little heart. Soon after that desperate prayer, Bracey fell asleep in my arms. It truly was a blessing given by God. The nurses came for him. It was finally time.

I was allowed to carry him to the operating room doors. Torrey and I hugged and kissed our little sleeping boy one more time, then handed him to the nurse. Bracey only stirred a little bit. The nurse and anesthesiologist were able to put Bracey under without him ever really waking up. My heart was full of joy. Stopping at that red line and handing your baby over to a nurse while he's crying and reaching for you is heartbreaking. My mighty God allowed Bracey to rest and calmly go into the operating room.

Waiting in the waiting room is draining. Torrey and I were lucky to be surrounded by family. They were a good distraction. We were told the surgery would be anywhere from four to five hours, but after only two and a half hours, we were called back to speak with the doctor. Everything had gone great! Most importantly, Bracey's breathing was great. They did not have to fully intubate. Bracey was able to breathe by using a LMA (laryngeal mask airway) so nothing went down his trachea. The doctor was able to place the external fixator and perform the pollicization on the right hand without any complications.

Torrey and I went into the recovery room while Bracey was still asleep. Bracey had a cast on his right arm, so we could not see the fixator yet; however, we could see the tip of his new thumb! I crawled up in bed with him, and he slowly turned his head toward me and whispered, "Hi, Mommy." Oh, my heart melted. I was still on the bed with him when they rolled us to Bracey's room. We would stay the night for observation.

Family was still there for company even though Bracey slept most of the evening and night. He didn't want to be put down, so we all took turns holding him. The next morning, Bracey was alert, asking for food, and he didn't seem to be in much pain. We were discharged late that morning.

We spent the next few days at my parents' house since it

was much closer to Bracey's doctors than our house. Bracey was having some pain, and the doctor was able to order additional pain medicine. By day four post-op, Bracey, being the strong, brave, life-loving little boy that he is, was back to jumping, running, and eating again.

July 29, 2011—Three Years Old

Eleven days had passed since Bracey's surgery, and it was time to remove the cast. We drove down to his doctor's office in Indianapolis. Bracey was a little nervous. He wasn't in pain but was just anxious about the removal of the cast. He sat on my lap as the doctor unwrapped the cast layer by layer. Tears rolled down my cheeks as his cast came off; for the first time in Bracey's life, he had a thumb, and his arm was straight. When the cast came off, we saw two pins in his thumb and an external fixator in both his hand and arm with six metal bars. I was just in awe. I am amazed and grateful for modern medicine.

The doctor demonstrated how to care for his arm and hand. Each day, we were to lengthen the fixator. We were to turn the dial 180 degrees, and slowly Bracey's arm would continue to grow longer. The doctor assured us it would not hurt, but Bracey certainly felt it. Every time, I had to distract him as Torrey turned the dial. Bracey whimpered and said his boo-boo hurt.

After a few weeks, we noticed the dial on his fixator was no longer turning properly. Bracey was already scheduled for the next surgery. They were going to do the same procedure on his left hand, so the doctor wanted to wait and check the right arm's hardware at that time. He would also remove the pins from Bracey's right thumb.

September 1, 2011—Three and a Half Years Old

Surgery day was upon us again. Bracey was going to get a thumb on his left hand, and his left forearm would be lengthened by fixators. The doctor was also going to look at the right fixator and remove Bracey's pins from his thumb. Even though I was overwhelmed by the same feelings and emotions I felt just a little over a month before, I knew we were doing the right thing. In a few months, Bracey would have full use of both his arms and hands again. He was going to do great.

Halfway through the surgery, the doctor came out to speak with us. He said Bracey was doing great and his left hand looked beautiful. His right fixator, however, was not able to be repaired. He said he would have to remove it and put in a new one. He explained all of the complications we would face by changing out the hardware so soon after having it put in. The doctor said he would finish up Bracey's left hand and give us a few minutes to talk it over.

We prayed about it, and we did not have peace about replacing the hardware at that time. Not replacing the hardware would mean we could not continue to lengthen Bracey's right arm. The broken fixator would remain in his arm until the doctor felt it was time to remove it. He would not get any more length in his right arm, but we had peace about our decision, and the doctor seemed to feel we made a good decision also.

Bracey came out of the surgery like a champ. He was more

alert this time than after his surgery back in July. We felt comfortable enough to take him home that very afternoon. His numbing medication wore off in the middle of the night, and he became very upset. We started him on the pain medicine given by the doctor. We set our alarms and kept on top of the doses to make sure it didn't wear off. Nevertheless, Bracey was miserable. He went forty-eight hours in excruciating pain. He didn't want to open his eyes. He wouldn't eat or drink. Nothing made him comfortable. Those two days seemed like a lifetime.

By day four, Bracey had developed a terrible cough, and a respiratory infection had set in. It was September 5, and he hadn't had a respiratory infection since late spring. But with fall upon us, it was inevitable. Bracey was bound to get sick. We began his breathing treatments every four hours, and his pulmonologist started him on a round of steroids and antibiotics. After just a few days, Bracey was feeling much better. His pain had greatly decreased, and his cough was controlled. We managed another recovery at home.

September 13, 2011—Three and a Half Years Old

Bracey's cast on his left hand came off. It was exciting to see that he now had two thumbs! We went home with instructions on how to start lengthening the fixator on his left arm. Bracey was doing great. He didn't seem to have any pain this time when we turned the dial. It was much different from the experience we had with his right hand. For the next couple of weeks, we continued to clean the area and lengthen his left arm.

We noticed Bracey's left thumb looked different than his

thumb on his right hand. We went back in to see the doctor on September 30. The doctor explained the finger that sits next to his thumb is a nonworking finger. He thought it would inhibit Bracey's new thumb from working properly. He suggested we remove this nonworking finger.

Seriously, we were supposed to make the decision to remove our son's finger? How could we make this decision? Although he has never had full movement or control of his fingers, they still serve a purpose. Bracey has only ever had complete full control of his pinkies. His other fingers didn't quite work, but Bracey was in hand therapy, and we hoped his hands and fingers would work and be useful to him as he continued to grow and adapt. We decided to not remove any fingers but to allow him to figure out how to adapt.

October 23, 2011—Three and a Half Years Old

Bracey was scheduled for the removal of his external fixators, but he developed a respiratory infection, and the surgery had to be rescheduled. Although Bracey was in the prime time of the year for his respiratory infections, we had been catching them early and were proactive in treating them. We were able to control the infections from home, but we still had to push his surgery back another week.

November 10, 2011—Three and a Half Years Old

Bracey was finally healthy enough to have surgery to remove both his external fixators and thumb pins. No matter how minor the procedures are, that red line still gets me. We have come to know the nurses in the pre-op rooms, and they have a tremendous team of people who bring toys and play with the children before surgery; then that specific person typically takes the child back to surgery. Nevertheless, I still get a nauseous ache in the pit of my stomach every time I hug and kiss Bracey at that red line.

After a mere forty-five minutes, Bracey was out of surgery. It had seemed like such a long four months, but it was finally over. Bracey was rid of his fixators and thumb pins. His right arm would always be shorter than the left, due to the complications we had with his fixator, but overall, we were very happy with the outcome of his surgeries. He had to wear braces on both arms, only at night, and just for two weeks. Then his therapy could start back up. He was so happy to have unhindered use of his arms again.

December 2011—Three and a Half Years Old

Another December came, filled with all the usual holiday festivals. Bracey had begun his hand therapy, and although there were times he didn't like it, he was doing well. He was learning how to use his new thumbs. He worked on pinching and picking things up. He was doing great!

In January, his therapist mentioned to me Bracey's right hand looked different. She thought it looked like it was curved in quite a bit. I thought I had noticed this, but, being the paranoid mom I can be, I hadn't made a big deal about it. The fact she brought it up to me confirmed my suspicions. I made an effort to really watch Bracey as he played during the next week and noticed he wasn't really using his right hand at all. He had been right-hand dominant, and now he wasn't using it. I was concerned and knew in my heart what this meant. In late January, I contacted the doctor and made an appointment.

January 30, 2012—Almost Four Years Old

We headed back down to Indy to meet with the doctor. After a thorough examination and x-ray, the doctor informed us Bracey's ulna had fused with his humerus at a ninety-degree angle. He could not explain why this had happened but said he would need to perform an ulnar nonunion repair. He would cut and break the bone away from the humerus and needed to place internal rods and screws to hold the ulna straight out. This was devastating news to me. I thought we were done with hand/arm surgeries. I didn't understand how this could have happened and why, unfortunately, the doctor couldn't explain either. Because this wasn't life-threatening and it wouldn't further hinder Bracey's hand, we put the surgery off until after the winter season. Putting Bracey through surgery in the winter was not a good option.

Bracey's right hand went from being dominant to unusable.

For most people, this would be devastating, but not for our boy. He, like always, adapted. He learned very quickly how to depend on his left hand and used his right elbow to help pick things up. To this day, Bracey is left-handed.

February 6, 2012—Four Years Old

Bracey celebrated his fourth birthday! He wanted to go to Cracker Barrel for his celebration dinner. That evening at the Barrel, Bracey didn't seem to feel well. He didn't want to eat. When Bracey doesn't want to eat, especially at his favorite restaurant, we know he's getting sick. Later that evening, Bracey looked miserable. His oxygen levels were in the low nineties. That next morning, I took him to his local pediatrician's office, hoping to again treat this infection at home. The x-rays indicated bilateral pneumonia. I called Bracey's pulmonologist, and she wanted to see him right away. So, I packed up a few things in case she admitted him, and off to Indy we went.

The pulmonologist said she didn't feel like it was bilateral pneumonia but would like to run a few tests. Due to the development of Bracey's body, his lungs look different than most lungs. She did not like the way his lungs sounded or looked on the x-rays. She wanted a sleep study and a scope of his trachea and lungs. That would, of course, need to wait until summer, as neither of us wanted him in the hospital during the winter if possible. She treated him for his respiratory infection, and we went home that evening. We had an oximeter at the house so we could monitor his oxygen levels when needed. We began the around-the-clock breathing treatments.

April 20, 2012—Four Years Old

Bracey was showing his typical signs of another respiratory infection setting in. I spoke with his doctor that morning, and she called in a prescription for him. He was acting lethargic. I put him down for a nap at noon, and when Torrey got home at four o'clock, he was still napping. I checked on him several times. He was just sleeping away. I felt it best to just let his body sleep and, hopefully, heal.

When we got Bracey up to do his breathing treatment, he sounded terrible. He had a fever of 102, and his oxygen level was at 85 percent. Torrey and I knew he needed medical attention. I packed up very quickly, and Bracey and I went down to our ER in Indy. I called the on-call doctor on my way so they could give the ER a heads-up we were coming. I admit that I did cautiously speed that evening. Bracey slept the entire way. Still an hour away from the hospital, we ran into heavy traffic. We were barely moving. I thought seriously about calling 911 to ask if they would escort me the rest of the way, but after about fifteen minutes, the traffic flow started picking up again.

Once finally there, we were met by my parents, which always made Bracey happy. He just wanted Pawpaw to carry him. We were quickly taken back to a room they had prepared for us. Bracey's oxygen was down to 81 percent. He was put on oxygen, and they started a double breathing treatment right away. They admitted him, as expected. After twenty-four hours of steroids, antibiotics, and breathing treatments every two hours, Bracey was doing much better. He was able to come off the oxygen, and his treatments went from every two hours to every three hours.

Bracey and I knew that as soon as his body was able to go four hours between breathing treatments, he would get to go home. And, on April 23, we were able to go home. We continued his breathing treatments at home until his cough was completely gone.

June 2012—Four Years Old

The summer of 2012 was finally upon us. Torrey and I had been planning on a big Mullins family vacation (just the adults) for a couple of years. All four of his siblings and their spouses and his parents were going on a cruise. As exciting as this was for us, I hated the thought of leaving my kids.

Until that summer, I had not left my kids for longer than a night or so at a time. However, Torrey and I needed this time away together. Our marriage was strong, but we rarely spent time alone. This vacation was just what we needed. Even though I knew that, it was tough to say goodbye to my babies. I knew they were in great hands with my parents. My heart still ached a bit inside.

They had a blast at their grandparents'. They were surrounded with cousins, and I'm sure they didn't miss me at all. Although getting away was emotional for me, it was so good for me and our marriage. I enjoyed every moment of vacation together.

Coming home to those sweet faces was amazing. I had missed their little hugs and kisses. I had missed their smiles and the sound of their laughter.

Being home meant preparing for Bracey's next surgery. Summer was typically a good time for Bracey, so we scheduled his third hand surgery for July. I was very much dreading this surgery. I was upset his hand surgeries had not ended up as I had planned, and I began to let it build up anger in my heart. I hated the thought of putting Bracey through another hand surgery. Another heartbreaking moment of handing him off to the nurse at that wretched red line. Another restless time of waiting in the waiting room for the doctor to tell us everything had gone well. Another time of painful recovery and more sleepless nights. Another time for therapy and learning a new way of doing things with his right hand. I was beginning to regret we ever had his hand corrected in the first place.

As the day approached, I grew more and more anxious. Torrey noticed my irritability the day before his surgery. He took me aside and asked how I was feeling. I shared with him my hurting heart. I told him it wasn't fair for Bracey to have to go through another painful surgery and recovery. When was it going to stop? When was my heart going to stop hurting and aching for him? Why did God continue to bring such trials and challenges to Bracey's life? Hasn't Bracey been through enough? Did we make the wrong decision when we agreed to correct his hands? Maybe that was not what God wanted for Bracey. God created him the way God wanted him, and who were we to change that? Why did we ever go down this path?

Torrey held my hands and reminded me God chose us to be his parents. God knew we would decide to help correct Bracey's hands. God knew Bracey's hand would not heal properly. God knew Bracey would be having another hand surgery. God knew all of Bracey's ailments before he was born. He could have given Bracey to other parents, but He chose us. God knew we would have tough decisions to face in Bracey's life. We have already made some of those decisions. All we could do was ask God to direct us to the best doctors for Bracey and give us peace about the decisions we made.

Torrey gave me perspective that evening and reminded me that four years ago, I gave Bracey to the Lord. He was not mine. I was merely the tool God was using to help raise and shape this precious boy. I was not always good at it, and I failed at times, but I daily worked at being the best mother I could be for both of our children.

July 19, 2012—Four Years Old

Surgery day arrived. As usual, Bracey was happy. He built block towers with Pawpaw as we waited in the pre-op room. Just before the nurse came in to take Bracey away, Bracey asked me if it would hurt. Talk about swallowing back your tears!

Bracey had never really asked about his surgeries before. We always explained to him what was going to happen and what to expect. This was the first time he was old enough to wonder ahead of time what was going to happen. I told him he wouldn't feel the surgery because he would be asleep and have great dreams. I told him I would be right beside him when he woke up. I told him he might be a little sore after the surgery, but the doctors would give us medicine to help him with the soreness. He just smiled and said, "Okay."

After two lingering hours in that waiting room, the doctor finally came out and said Bracey did great! They were able to unfuse his bones and straighten his hand with a small internal plate and five screws. The doctor said he placed a protective cast on Bracey's arm, and he would remove it at the two-week checkup. I thanked him, and the nurse took me to Bracey.

Bracey was already a bit alert and asked for Pawpaw. I smiled at him and explained Pawpaw couldn't come back yet, but I would get him just as soon as I could.

After those first few happy moments, it didn't take long for Bracey's pain to set in. By the time we were home that evening, Bracey was in a great deal of pain. We gave him the pain medicine prescribed by his doctor, and he finally fell asleep. I noticed a little bit of swelling in his fingers but figured that was normal.

July 27, 2012—Four Years Old

Eight days after surgery, on a Friday afternoon, Bracey's cast fell off. His arm was very swollen. I called the doctor, and he told me it shouldn't still be swollen. He asked me to wrap Bracey's arm to protect the sutures and to keep Bracey from playing too much over the weekend, and he would see Bracey Monday.

Thankfully, my sister-in-law, Tenisha, was able to come and visit for a few days. She stayed with Brynn while I made the trip down to Indy on Monday.

The doctor thought Bracey's arm was healing nicely. The swelling was finally going down, and the x-ray looked great. He was impressed with the straightness of his arm. Bracey had noticed it too and pointed it out to me by comparing his two arms. The doctor thought maybe the cast had been a bit too tight, which caused the swelling. The doctor agreed to keep the cast off as long as I kept the sutures covered for another week.

After six hand surgeries, we were ready to move on and begin therapy for his thumbs. We spent the next several months in weekly occupational therapy. Bracey quickly learned his own way of doing things with his hands. He has always adapted to whatever life brings him. He has always been determined to do anything others can do.

August 2012—Four Years Old

Summer was quickly coming to an end, and we were gearing up for Bracey to begin preschool. Preschool! How was it Bracey could be old enough for preschool? We were so excited and nervous. I was excited to watch Bracey make new friends and continue to develop his motor skills.

We were one week out from starting school, and—wouldn't you know it—Bracey developed a respiratory infection. We did his usual routine of increased breathing treatments, shaking therapy vest, added steroids, and lots of rest. We needed to kick this infection before school started. After two days of intense therapy and medications, I could tell he was on the mend. His cough was junky, but at least he was coughing it all up. His chest was loosening, and his personality was coming back.

Bracey was able to attend the school that Torrey had been working at. We also decided it was time for me to go back to work part-time. That same school, Victory Christian Academy, happened to have a part-time position available as well. It was a tough decision to go back into the working field, but at that time, we knew it was what was best. Torrey and I felt blessed to have jobs at the same school as Bracey. It was reassuring to know we were close by if Bracey or the teacher were to need us.

So, on August 23, 2012, Bracey began preschool, right on time. Bracey, like a lot of new students, was hesitant. It was tough for both of us. The second day was the worst. Bracey's sweet teacher had to carry him into the classroom because he wouldn't let go of me. I left him crying that morning, and I was swallowing back tears myself. Shortly after I left him, his amazing teacher texted me a picture of him playing and smiling. Nothing reassures a mama more than knowing her children are safe and are in a loving, caring environment.

When I went to pick up Bracey that day, his teacher told me Bracey was having great difficulty getting his crayons in and out of the crayon box. So, she had *all* the students take all of their crayons out of the cardboard boxes and put them in their pencil boxes. She threw all the little crayon boxes away. As a tiny four-year-old, just starting out in school, this was brilliant for Bracey's self-esteem. I am sure it made crayon time much easier for all the children and teachers as well. I knew that day that Bracey was in the best place for him. He had caring, loving, and patient teachers.

Bracey quickly developed his own way of holding pencils, crayons, and markers. He was determined to prove he could do things the other boys and girls were doing. His teachers quickly learned some of Bracey's particular challenges, and I was able to get adaptive tools for him. He used a rubber mat to help keep his papers from slipping while he drew. He used special pencil grips. It was a year of trial and error. Some things worked, while some did not. Cutting paper was very difficult for him. We got some special scissors, but they did not work well for him. We got a kid's safe cutting board, but it was just awkward for him. Cutting things out was a challenge for him, but we continued to work on it.

Fall of 2012 came, as did Bracey's typical fall respiratory infections. Bracey woke up on September 26, 2012, with a fever and full-blown respiratory infection. Thankfully, his pulmonologist was able to see him that very day. She started the usual routine and added an antibiotic to cover his lungs. He was out of school the rest of that week but was able to rest and heal from home. His entire class made a sweet card for Bracey to cheer him up. He had recovered by the next week and was back at school.

Despite the onset of respiratory infection season, we loved autumn around our home. We were privileged to live right by an amazing apple orchard. It was our tradition to go at least once during the season and take the kids, along with our friends, to the orchard. We took the tractor ride to pick apples from the orchard and got a box of their famous doughnuts. It was always such a sweet day for us as a family.

That fall, Bracey also had the honor of being a ring bearer for some dear friends in New York. Bracey had a minor cough and was developing another infection, but we began to treat it, and he was an irresistible little ring bearer. He had the sweetest little tux, and the bride agreed to let him wear a top hat he wanted. He did great walking down that aisle with the sweetest little princess. Once he got to the front, however, he realized he was in front of a lot of people. He wanted to come and sit with us. Just as I was about to get up and stop him from ruining this precious couple's wedding, the groomsman pulled out a little bag of skittles and enticed Bracey to stay up there with him. It was so perfect. Bracey sat there on that step, so quietly, eating Skittles one at a time. It was priceless.

November 20, 2012—Four Years Old

I got a call from Bracey's school saying he had fallen off a tricycle at recess and busted his mouth pretty good. I was in the middle of teaching a class, and Torrey had some free time, so he went to see how Bracey was doing.

Torrey called and said he needed to take Bracey to the dentist, because his tooth looked bad. After looking, the pediatric dentist sent Bracey on to a pediatric dental specialist. The specialist said the affected tooth had cracked in half and would probably fall out early, but it should be just fine. So, our brave little boy with a busted mouth went back to school the next day.

Just a couple days later was Thanksgiving, and we traveled to our extended family's house. During the break, Bracey complained repeatedly his mouth hurt. We gave him Tylenol periodically, but his gum looked like it was swelling in between the crack of his tooth. The Tuesday after Thanksgiving, we took Bracey back to the dentist, and he decided Bracey needed surgery because his nerves were exposed and his tooth needed to come out. He sent us down to Indy to see yet another specialist.

The specialist was able to see us the very next day. He did an x-ray and said Bracey had an infection he wanted to treat before the surgery. His nerves were exposed and could be painful for him. He wanted to do surgery as soon as possible, but the infection had to be treated first. He scheduled the surgery for the following Thursday, and we went home with pain medicine and an antibiotic.

December 6, 2012—Four Years Old

The infection had subsided, so another surgery day had arrived. Torrey was unable to be with us for this surgery, but my dad was able to come. And we all know, Pawpaw was second best to dad. The nurses came to get Bracey, and he walked back willingly. He was growing up. He just grabbed the nurse's hand, let us kiss him, and off he went, telling the nurse all about his tricycle accident. That did my heart good.

The nurse came out a short time later and said Bracey was doing well but his oxygen started dropping a bit, so they had to intubate him. It always made for a more difficult recovery when Bracey was intubated. His trachea just didn't handle that well. An hour went by before the doctor came out and said he was doing great. He removed Bracey's tooth, stitched up the open nerve, and even filled a cavity they found. He said Bracey should get his adult tooth at the expected time, and he didn't feel like the accident had done any damage to the roots. He said Bracey was awake and asked for me.

It was so good to see him smiling as my dad and I walked into Bracey's room. The first thing he said was he was hungry. That's always a good sign. We had a special lunch with Pawpaw and then headed home.

One week later, December 13, I could tell Bracey wasn't feeling well. His teacher also reported he had his head down most of the morning. We began our normal routine for Bracey's respiratory infections. Late that evening, Bracey woke up and needed to throw up. Throwing up has always been challenging for Bracey. When he throws up, his trachea collapses, which causes airflow to momentarily stop. Because of Bracey's previous TEF surgical repair, his esophagus was narrower than most people's, and that made throwing up more difficult as well. In that moment,

Bracey cannot breathe. We keep Bracey calm, and he is able to take a breath again shortly after throwing up. When Bracey had a severe respiratory infection, he tended to throw up mucus a lot. I knew that night he needed to see his pulmonologist.

His doctor saw him the next morning. She confirmed he had bilateral pneumonia. She said she was comfortable with me treating him at home as long as I kept an eye on his oxygen levels. Bracey did not bounce back quickly from this bout of infection. He continued to have fevers for a week. He was miserable. He didn't want to do anything. We were doing treatments every four hours, even through the night. Torrey and I traded off the nighttime breathing treatments. We were exhausted. Bracey just didn't seem to get better. He missed the rest of December at school. He was sick for two solid weeks. Even after his fevers were completely gone, he was still coughing and felt miserable.

Christmas was upon us, and we decided to make the trip to my parents' house. We felt like Bracey needed a good distraction, and the grandparents' house was just the place. Bracey was so happy to be at Mama and Pawpaw's house. For the first time in more than two weeks, he smiled and played. His cough continued to linger, but his happy spirit was back.

After Christmas, Bracey's cough seemed to get worse again. We had never seen this before. Usually after aggressive treatments, Bracey recovered and had a couple months before he would get sick again. His respiratory infections had never regressed after such strenuous treatments. His doctor wanted to see us again. So, on December 28, we made another trip down to Indy.

Bracey's oxygen was sitting right at 93 percent. She continued to listen to him, and she had a worried look on her face. She listened a bit longer than usual. She finally looked at me with concern and solemnly relayed Bracey had very little airflow in his left lung. She added a new inhaler to his regimen of medications. It was a steroid inhaler to help open up his airways and keep them open longer. She wanted to be aggressive with her treatment. The rest of Christmas break, we stayed inside, trying to get Bracey back to his baseline before school started back up again.

January 2013—Almost Five Years Old

School was back in session. Bracey was doing better, and it seemed as if his new medication was helping him. He had missed school for most of December, and he was ready to get back with his friends and teachers. Despite all of his physical struggles, Bracey was still a typical little boy. On January 12, his teacher told me Bracey had gotten in a little bit of trouble that day. I sat down with Bracey that afternoon and asked him what happened at school. He said he and some friends were building towers with blocks, and his friend was not taking turns and was not sharing, so he knocked his tower over. I expressed the importance of showing kindness and being patient. After our little talk, I asked him what he could do differently the next time. He said, "I will tell my teacher and let her knock his tower down."

February 27, 2013—Five Years Old

The stomach bug hit Bracey hard. The sound of my little guy using every muscle possible to throw up was heart-wrenching. His little body worked hard to throw up, yet nothing would come out. He was miserable. He was shaking, weak, and lethargic. I gave him tiny sips of liquid, but he threw up almost immediately. He continued like this for twenty-four hours. His legs were hard as rocks. He could not stand or walk. His feet were pointed inward. I knew he was very dehydrated. So, off to the local ER we went. They gave him intravenous fluids, which he received without flinching. His blood work came back severely dehydrated. After four hours of intravenous fluids and nausea medication, Bracey and I went home. I don't know what it was about that nausea medication, but it worked incredibly fast. Bracey recovered within a couple of days of getting the IV fluids and meds. He went back to school and finished out his first year of preschool.

The summer of 2013 came with many decisions. Torrey and I had decided that my working, even part-time, was too much on our family. I had missed a lot of work that school year due to Bracey's health, and that wasn't fair to the school. The school was also not going to be able to offer Torrey a full load of classes, and therefore we had to decide what additional work he would be able to do. God's timing was perfect! Another Christian school, Portage Christian School, was looking for an athletic director, and Torrey was offered that position.

That summer flew by as always. August 2013 came, and Bracey headed off to kindergarten, and it was my baby girl's turn to go to preschool. It was such an emotional time for me.

I choked back the tears as I dropped both of my babies off at school.

September 2013—Five Years Old

Bracey developed a minor cough just in time for a routinely scheduled checkup with his pulmonologist. The doctor was still not hearing much air flow through his left lung, but Bracey's body adapted, and his oxygen levels were staying above ninety. We went home and began every-four-hour breathing treatments during the day, trying to combat his cough.

October 2013—Five Years Old

Bracey's cough remained. It had been almost four weeks with a continued cough. He missed a lot of school, as his coughing was getting more aggressive and caused him to gag. On October 18, we made another trip down to Indy. Bracey was not getting better, and he needed to see his doctor.

His consistent, aggressive coughs caused both his GI doctor and his pulmonary doctor to feel like he could have developed another TEF (tracheoesophageal fistula) or a tear in his previous TEF repair sight. The doctors agreed to do a barium swallow study test first before a scope procedure. So, on October 28, 2013, we had the barium swallow study done to try to rule out a TEF or tear. The study did not show anything conclusive, so the doctors went ahead and scheduled an endoscopy and bronchoscopy.

November 12, 2013—Five Years Old

Bracey had his scopes done. As with any procedure, we kissed our little boy and stopped at the red line while the nurses took Bracey back to the operating room. Bracey was definitely growing up. Familiar with the process, it was easy for him to go with the nurse. He knew his throat would be a little sore when he woke up, but he really shouldn't be in much pain.

It was only about forty-five minutes until the doctors called us back. Bracey's GI doctor told us his stomach was full of liquid. Bracey hadn't had anything to eat or drink in over eighteen hours, so it should have been completely empty. She said his stomach was obviously not emptying itself. He also had a couple of polyps near his stomach, which she sent off to be biopsied. She decided because of his struggles with motility in his esophagus and now his stomach as well, she wanted to start him on medication to help him with this poor motility. The new medication would help his food move down to his stomach and help his stomach muscles extract the food out of his stomach.

Next came the report from his pulmonologist. She looked concerned and said Bracey really did not tolerate her scope. His trachea kept collapsing on her camera, so they had to give him breaks to allow his oxygen to come back up. She said the right lung looked great. There was a little bit of mucus in his right lung, so she suctioned that out. She was able to look inside every chamber, and it looked like a nice, healthy lung.

However, she explained she was unable to look in Bracey's left lung, as it was collapsed, and she could not get her scope in the lung. She said there was very little airflow from the left lung. She could see his curved spine (congenital scoliosis—the V from VACTERL) was pressing on the lung, which was probably the cause of his chronic cough. After what they saw in his scopes, his doctors were amazed Bracey had managed to stay out of the hospital through numerous respiratory infections and keep his oxygen levels up. I told them Bracey's body had always adapted to whatever life brought him. God had a special plan for Bracey, and whatever came, Bracey was ready for the challenge.

December 4, 2013—Five Years Old

Just three weeks after Bracey's scopes, he started to fight another respiratory infection. Bracey's respiratory infections were coming more frequently. I knew in my heart he couldn't continue like this. His body was continuously fighting off infection, and his right lung was working overtime to make up for the weak left lung.

This latest infection caused great exhaustion for Bracey. He slept off and on for two days before I could get him in to see his doctor. His oxygen was bouncing between 92 and 93 percent. His doctor, yet again, listened to him and looked up at me with such concern on her face. She didn't even have to say anything. I knew. I didn't want to hear her say it. Bracey's lung function was not good.

Before she could say a word, I turned away from her and Bracey and started crying. I had never cried in her office before, and I had never cried in front of Bracey. I never wanted Bracey to feel like he made me sad. *He* certainly has not. I was sad because I knew what her look meant. She placed her hand on my shoulder, and I turned around, and she gave me a hug. She said it was time to start talking about what was next for Bracey. He could not continue to have these infections. His left lung was not functioning now, and it was because his spine was pressing against it. She stated that, without intervention, he could lose his left lung, and his spine would begin to press on his heart.

I just looked at her, and with tears running down my face, I said, "I can't put him through another surgery." She was very comforting and assured me this was the absolute best thing for him. If we wanted to give him the best pulmonary care, we had to begin looking at correcting his congenital scoliosis.

When Bracey was in the NICU, his doctors had told us about his congenital scoliosis and hemivertebrae. They did not know his prognosis at that time but said it would most likely need to be corrected as he got older.

I thanked our trusted doctor for her compassion and love for Bracey, and we headed home. As we drove home, Bracey was enjoying some nuggets from our favorite chicken restaurant, and he began to cough. I reminded him to take a drink, and I looked back and could tell he needed help. He had panic in his eyes. I quickly pulled off onto the shoulder and ran around to help him. I got him out of the car seat as quickly and calmly as possible and helped him get the food out. He was able to throw it up after a few pats on the upper back. I squeezed him tightly.

I told him I was so sorry he had to go through this, but Daddy and I were going to work hard to get the perfect doctors to help him. I put him back in his car seat, shut his door, and cried.

"Thank You, Lord, for allowing me to be able to safely pull over and help Bracey. Thank You for Your daily protection over us."

That evening, I filled Torrey in on everything the doctor had said. We both agreed it was time to seek an orthopedic surgeon for Bracey. Another surgery for Bracey—and not just a surgery, a major surgery. I sat on our bed that evening, and as tears rolled down my cheeks, Torrey sat beside me, wrapped his arms around me, and reminded me again God is in control. He has always been in control and will always be in control. God already knew Bracey would need back surgery, and God already knew who his surgeon would be, even though we did not. God had huge plans for Bracey. We had to do everything we could to find that doctor.

December 17, 2013—Five Years Old

We began Bracey's back journey on December 17, 2013. We met with a pediatric orthopedic doctor in Indianapolis. He was a very kind man. He took x-rays of Bracey's back and examined them. He told us he thought Bracey's back was measuring around fifty-seven-degree curvature, but there was not an exact science to measuring the curve, so it could be off a bit. His opinion was that, with a curvature of roughly fifty-seven degrees, it did not warrant surgery. He did not believe Bracey's spine could be causing his lung issues. He did not think Bracey's spine was pressing on his lungs. The doctor went on to say if the spine were to press on his lung, it would be pressing on the right lung rather than the left lung.

I called our pulmonologist the next morning to talk with her about what the orthopedic doctor said. She did not say too much other than suggesting we search for a second opinion if we didn't agree with the doctor.

December 21, 2013

A few days later, our pulmonologist called me to talk about Bracey. She told me she met with a couple other pulmonary specialists about Bracey's condition, and the other doctors agreed with her that his spine needed to be corrected in order to improve his lung function. She strongly encouraged us to get a second opinion. She was convinced Bracey's spine was pressing against his left lung. She had been with Bracey since he was six months old. She had seen him at his absolute best and his worst. She had seen his insides with her own eyes. She had loved him as if he were her own child. We trusted her completely. If she suggested we get a second opinion, then that was exactly what we would do.

So, we went back to the drawing board. We researched doctors and contacted our insurance to see who was in our network. It sounded simple, but it was not a simple process.

Christmas of 2013 was a great Christmas. We knew we had our work cut out for us to find the right doctor for Bracey. Even though we had many unanswered questions about Bracey's future, we had a great network of family, friends, and doctors there to encourage us and give us direction.

After the new year, I amped up the search, trying to find the best doctor out there for Bracey. I remembered a doctor who had evaluated Bracey while he was an infant in the NICU in Chicago. I called that hospital and tracked down that doctor. I spoke with his nurse to tell her briefly about Bracey's health and that we were looking for a second opinion. The doctor agreed to look at our case even though he would be out of network for our insurance.

January 30, 2014—Almost Six Years Old

The morning of January 30 came, and I was hopeful and anxious to meet with our second orthopedic surgeon to discuss Bracey's condition. As we walked back into the hospital that saved Bracey's life, there were so many emotions flooding my heart. I will forever be grateful to the amazing nurses and doctors who saved my son's life. I walked through the doors and was immediately reminded of the countless hours, days, weeks, and months we spent there.

The clean, crisp smell of the entryway brought me back to February 7, 2008. Memories of pulling up to that hospital after just having Bracey and being met by family members who were already there waiting for us. Memories of those elevators that took me up to where Bracey was being cared for in the NICU. Memories of holding my frail, sick baby for the first time and not wanting to let go. Memories of the doctors walking in and telling me why Bracey was sick and how they were going to save him. Memories of complete devastation but also hope and love. I will forever cherish these memories and how this hospital changed our lives.

Two hours went by, and we were finally able to see the doctor and get some answers. However, they weren't the answers we were hoping for. The doctor agreed with our first orthopedic doctor. He did not believe Bracey's congenital scoliosis could be causing him such breathing difficulties. He did not feel like his curved spine was pressing on his lung. I told him I truly appreciated him taking time out to see us, but Bracey's lung health was decreasing rapidly, and I believed in my heart it was because of his scoliosis.

I obviously had zero medical background history other than those past six years of being my son's personal nurse, but when I saw his x-ray, it just made sense his spine was pressing on his lung. His pulmonologist believed it to be true, as did her colleagues she had conferenced with. If I didn't fight for Bracey, he would be at risk of losing his lung—or worse, his spine would crush his heart.

So, back to the drawing board again for our little guy. I was even more determined to find a doctor who would listen to me and at least acknowledge the possibility of his spine crushing Bracey's lung.

February 6, 2014—Bracey Is Six Years Old!

For Bracey's sixth birthday, we reserved a hotel room near my parents' house. and all his cousins were going to come and have a fun winter pool party. Bracey started coughing and wheezing the evening before his party. We hit his breathing treatments hard that evening, trying to get ahead of any oncoming infection. On February 7, the morning of his party, Bracey was scheduled for a regular checkup with his pulmonologist. He was still coughing, and it was a tight cough. I was happy to be seeing our trusted doctor because I knew she could help give some medication that would help Bracey. We were so excited that day. What kid wouldn't love a pool birthday party in the middle of winter? So, we headed to Indy with a quick stop at the doctor's. It was, however, anything but quick.

When we arrived at the doctor's office, I could tell Bracey

was working harder to breathe. His oxygen was resting right at 90 percent. The doctor came in and also noticed he was working a little bit too hard to breathe. I told her it had just started last night and we were hoping to start him on medicine because he had a big birthday pool party that evening.

I could tell by the look on her face she knew something we didn't. She lifted his shirt and showed me how Bracey's rib cage was retracting with each rapid breath. With tears in my eyes, I told her I had no clue. She was very sincere and apologetic as she told us Bracey needed to go down to the ER and be admitted to the hospital. Bracey's eyes filled up with huge tears. Great disappointment came over both of us. Our sweet doctor, knowing how heartbroken Bracey was, told us she would like Bracey to get one double breathing treatment, and then she would see how he was doing. Maybe he would bounce back quickly. With tears in both of our eyes, we headed down to the ER.

On the way down, Bracey was really struggling to breathe. The nurses scooped him up, and within seconds, Bracey was on oxygen. The nurses and doctors kept coming in and out to check on him. They had wheeled a crash cart into his room as a precaution. Everything seemed to be happening so quickly. Just an hour ago, we were headed into a great, fun birthday weekend. Now my son was lying in a hospital bed, hooked up to oxygen, monitors, and IVs and surrounded by doctors and nurses.

Inside, my heart was racing. I was terrified, but I had not only Bracey to keep calm but Brynn as well. She didn't understand what was happening. In the midst of talking to doctors and nurses, I was texting my mom and Torrey. Someone needed to come and get Brynn. She didn't need to be there. A nurse mentioned they were getting a room ready for Bracey, and as soon as he was stable enough, they would be sending him up to a room, and Brynn wouldn't be allowed up there right then. Thankfully, my mom was able to leave work and come get her.

After Bracey's double breathing treatment in the ER, he was able to be taken to his room. He was still on oxygen, and his breathing was still very labored. This respiratory infection had hit fast and hard. I thank God He put us in the perfect place at the perfect time. Bracey slept right though the transport from the ER to his room. They continued his breathing treatments every two hours. His pulmonologist came in at the end of her day to check on Bracey. His breathing was still labored, but he wasn't working nearly as hard to breathe. She said she wanted to continue his treatments every two hours through the night.

I couldn't sleep that night, and as I was sitting next to him, Bracey started mumbling something. I leaned over to him to hear what he was saying. It was all gibberish, but he felt like he was on fire. I had Torrey go and get his nurse to check his temp. Sure enough, he had spiked a fever. His temp was 103.6. The next morning though, he seemed to be breathing with more ease. He continued to be lethargic for the next twenty-four hours. He wasn't eating. He was sleeping a lot. He continued the breathing treatments every two hours and was still on oxygen.

February 10 was a tough day for us. After four days in the hospital, we decided it would be best for Torrey to take Brynn and go home. I missed Brynn terribly. My heart ached to see her and hold her. It was flu season at the hospital, so children under a certain age were not permitted on Bracey's floor. We did not know when Bracey would be able to come home.

He was still on oxygen at night, and on day four, the doctors put Bracey in isolation. I understand and appreciate isolation, but it is terrible. I couldn't take Bracey for wagon rides around the floor anymore. He wasn't allowed to leave his room, and anyone who came in had to suit up. It was a miserable way to recover. His doctors said until his fevers subsided, he would be in isolation.

By this time, he was only getting fevers at night. He would go all day without needing oxygen or without getting a fever, but then night came, and his fevers would return, and his oxygen levels would drop. I was up most of that night in isolation, just praying Bracey could sleep all night without needing his oxygen put back on. Bracey was able to wean from two hours between treatments to three hours between treatments. That meant he was closer to going home.

Bracey did great that next night. His oxygen never fell below 90 percent. His pulmonary doctor stopped in the next morning to see how Bracey was doing. She agreed to remove him from isolation and to stretch his breathing treatments to every four hours. Bracey was so happy. He knew moving his treatments to four-hour increments meant he was close to going home. He lit up. His entire demeanor changed that morning. He was determined to prove to his doctor he was ready to go home. With the isolation restrictions lifted, we went on walks around the floor. Bracey was still weak, so I pulled him around in a wagon. We must have done a dozen laps that morning.

February 11, 2014—Six Years Old

Late in the afternoon, on the fifth day of being in the hospital, the doctor came in and asked Bracey if he'd like to go home. We were so excited! We wanted nothing more than to go home. We both missed Torrey and Brynn. I packed up our room, and as soon as the discharge papers were ready, we headed home.

Being home was one of the best feelings in the world—a feeling of completeness, of renewed energy. I picked Brynn up, and she wrapped her little arms around me. I didn't want to let her go. We were a family once again.

Bracey's cough continued to linger. It seemed as if his cough was never going to go away. In fact, it seemed as if he was getting worse again. On February 26, just two weeks after being home from the hospital, I could tell health-wise Bracey was still not at his best. He wasn't able to kick this lingering infection, but he didn't have a fever, so off to school we went.

It was a bitter, cold morning. We bundled up as much as possible to keep Bracey from breathing the terribly cold air. I was helping out at the school that morning, and about forty-five minutes into the school day, Bracey's teacher brought him down to me. I knew right away he was working hard to breathe. I could see the fear in his eyes. I quickly gathered my things and, keeping him calm, drove Bracey straight to the ER. I walked in and told them he was having an asthma attack and needed a double treatment of albuterol right away. Telling the local ER that he was having an asthma attack was easier than having to explain what tracheomalacia was and his declining lung health. I knew the treatment would be the same, and it saved time.

We didn't even sit and wait. They took us straight back into the exam room. As they were hooking him up, I was able to get in touch with our pulmonologist on the phone, and she spoke with the doctor and gave him directions to treat him. Knowing she spoke with the ER doctor gave me such peace about Bracey's treatment there. After his double treatment, he started to breathe easier and rest. They sent him for a chest x-ray, and it showed pneumonia in his left lung. Per our pulmonary doctor, they started him on an oral steroid and an antibiotic to cover his lungs.

The ER doctor strongly encouraged me to drive straight down to Indy after his treatment. I knew if I drove him down to Indy, he would be placed back in the hospital again. I couldn't do that to him. The thought of spending more time in the hospital crushed me. I knew as long as his oxygen level stayed above 90 percent, I could handle his care from home. I spoke with his pulmonologist, and she was comfortable with us staying home as long I continued to monitor his oxygen.

He spent the next couple of days on the oximeter machine with around-the-clock breathing treatments as well as his therapy vest. Those were long days and nights, but I was determined to keep Bracey home. He slept in bed with me, as it was easier for me to keep an eye on his oxygen levels and continue his breathing treatments throughout the night without having to get him out of bed. His oxygen levels would occasionally drop below ninety while he was sleeping, but it would bounce back up after I'd readjust him. Three days after the ER visit, Bracey was feeling better, and I could tell he was on the mend.

March 2014 was finally upon us, and Bracey's breathing was better, but he continued to cough. His aggressive coughing subsided, and he was left with that same lingering, minor cough. He saw his pulmonologist in the middle of March. She was not happy with his lung function.

She was still very certain his lung function was decreasing due to his spine curvature. However, she wanted to rule out cystic fibrosis, as all of his symptoms could also be symptoms of CF. We had tried to rule it out once before, but the results came back inconclusive. Basically, to detect cystic fibrosis, the doctors measure the amount of sodium chloride in a person's sweat. This is called a sweat test. Before, they were unable to collect enough sweat. So, on April 18, 2014, we headed down to Indy to try to do yet another sweat test. The test came back invalid yet again. My little guy just can't seem to produce enough sweat for that test.

Meanwhile, his cough was increasing again, and he developed another fever. On April 21, 2014, I called his pulmonologist, and she got him in right away. On the way down to Indy, I could tell he was working hard to breathe again. I called the doctor's office and told her I felt like Bracey should just go straight to the ER. I did not know what his oxygen level was as I was driving, but I felt it was low.

Upon arrival, the nurses hooked him up, and his oxygen level was down to 84 percent. They put him on oxygen and started a breathing treatment. They called his pulmonologist, and she came down to see him. She agreed with the ER doctor that Bracey needed to be admitted. I had prepared myself for this possibility, and I had the foresight to prepare Bracey as well. I knew when our doctor listened to him, she would admit him. I knew he needed professional care. And so, once again, we began our routine of nurses, doctors, and respiratory therapists coming in our room every two hours. This time, our room was literally right across from the coffee machine. I'm pretty sure the Lord knew I would need this, as I was on my own this time.

We had decided it would be best for Torrey and Brynn to continue with their routine of school and work. I had packed a small bag just in case the doctor said we needed to stay. Bracey was responding quite quickly to the treatments. Within forty-eight hours of being admitted to the hospital, Bracey was well enough to come home.

Again, and still, Bracey's cough persisted. It did not seem to matter how many breathing treatments he had. His cough was not letting up. He had had this persistent cough since December 2013.

Just three weeks later, Bracey was sick again. We made the trip to his doctor in Indy. I felt like I would be able to treat this infection from home, and she agreed and sent us home with medications.

The cycle continued. The rest of May and June 2014, Bracey was coughing and choking. He coughed every time he ate. His choking episodes were becoming more and more frequent. I was growing more weary by the day. I felt helpless. I was even more determined to find the answers for Bracey. I made it my mission to research Bracey's condition. I talked with other mothers through blogs and telephone to find answers. Bracey needed an orthopedic doctor who would listen to us and help us figure out how to help Bracey.

July 2, 2014—Six Years Old

Bracey was sick yet again. He needed to see both his pulmonologist and his GI doctor. They were both able to get him in the next day. They both agreed it was time for Bracey to have another scope done. His pulmonologist did not think it would be wise to do another bronchoscopy, as he did not handle the last one very well. So this scope would be less invasive. We needed answers for his frequent choking episodes. He needed to be as healthy as possible before they could scope him. We continued doing around-the-clock breathing treatments and steroids to help clear out Bracey's lungs so he could get the endoscopy.

August 21, 2014—Six Years Old

Bracey had the test done. The doctor said it appeared his peristalsis muscles were still not working properly. He still had poor motility, even on the medication. His muscles were not pushing the food down his esophagus, nor were they clearing his stomach. He hadn't had anything to eat or drink for more than nineteen hours, yet his stomach was still full. The doctor started him on a different medication that would hopefully help with the poor motility. We were hopeful this would help with his choking episodes as well.

Meanwhile, I was still on my mission to find another orthopedic doctor. After six more months of research, including emailing doctors, speaking with families who had personal experience, and advice from our current team of doctors, we decided to seek out a pediatric orthopedic surgeon at a well-known orthopedic hospital in Chicago.

August 28, 2014—Six Years Old

Feeling optimistic and hopeful for Bracey's future, we headed into Chicago. The minute we walked into the hospital, we knew this was a sweet, special place for children. We were greeted with kindness and bright smiles. I handed the nurse my large binder of Bracey's history, including x-rays, scans, test results, medication lists, and doctors. You name it, it was in that binder. It was, in many ways, the story of Bracey's life thus far. I told her she could make copies of anything she needed. Shortly after, the doctor walked in. He spent a great deal of time with us. He listened to our concerns and looked through Bracey's medical history and x-rays. He was intrigued. He wanted to get fresh x-rays of Bracey's spine because it had been about ten months since his previous one. So, off to radiology we went.

We got back to the exam room, and the doctor came in with two x-rays, one from ten months ago and one from that day. He put the first one up on his white board and said it was from before. He was measuring him to be around fifty to fifty-two degrees curvature. Then he put that day's x-ray up and said he was measuring around seventy-degree curvature today. Instantly, it all clicked.

Bracey had hit a growth spurt in the last year and had been constantly sick in the past year. There was no doubt in my mind his constant illnesses were due to his growth spurt. It had increased his spinal curve, pressing more and more onto his left lung. The doctor explained with this significant increase in the curvature, we needed to prepare for surgery to correct his spine.

There were different types of scoliosis. Bracey's was congenital scoliosis, meaning he was born with it, as well as fused ribs and hemivertebrae. A back brace alone would not correct his spine. He would need internal rod(s) put in place to help correct the spine curvature. The doctor ordered a few more tests for Bracey, such as an MRI, an ultrasound of his kidneys, and an EKG. He said he would see us again and discuss more details once the tests were done.

We did not have to wait long before getting the tests done. The awesome orthopedic hospital was able to get everything scheduled, on the same day, within a couple of weeks. Due to Bracey's age, they needed to put him to sleep to perform the MRI. It would be a lengthy scan, and he needed to be completely still. I knew what the risks were for Bracey having to be sedated, even for something as simple as an MRI, but it needed to be done. It was time to move forward toward correcting his spine.

September 17, 2014—Six Years Old

The day of the additional testing was an especially emotional day for me. After nine months and three different orthopedic surgeons, I felt like we finally moved forward in getting the help Bracey needed to correct his spine and improve his overall lung health. I was anxious about Bracey being put to sleep again and the possibility of him being intubated. As we were waiting in the pre-op room, Bracey must have been able to feel my anxiety. He put his Legos down, looked up at me, and said, "Mommy, it's going to be a good day." I squeezed that little guy and thanked God for giving me such an incredible boy. My heart was filled with joy. I was stressed about things that had not even happened yet, and they weren't even happening to me! Bracey was the one going through all of this, yet he was the one calming and reassuring me. He truly is my brave gift from God.

The nurse came in and took us down to the MRI room where the doctor and technicians were waiting for us. They asked if we wanted to come in and hold Bracey's hand while he fell asleep. Absolutely, we did! I thought my heart was going to leap out of my chest with excitement. I took all of my jewelry off and stood there holding his hands while he calmly and peacefully fell asleep. I thanked the doctors for taking good care of him, and off to the waiting room we went.

Two very slow and long hours went by before the nurse came out and said Bracey was finished and was just waking up. We went into the post-op room, where he was already sitting up and talking. After thirty minutes, we were off to the ultrasound and EKG. We had a great, smooth day. Everything went perfectly, just as planned. We ended our action-packed day with a slushy, per Bracey's request!

October 2014—Six Years Old

In the midst of our overloaded, emotionally exhausted lives of illness after illness, doctor appointment after doctor appointment, hospitalization after hospitalization, test after test, some sweet anonymous person nominated Bracey for a Make-A-Wish trip. The Make-A-Wish foundation is a nonprofit organization that arranges experiences described as "wishes" to children diagnosed with critical illnesses. Bracey wished to go to Disney World in Florida. It was an incredible week for us as a family. A time for us to reconnect. A time for us to forget about all of those appointments, surgeries, and illnesses. Those six amazing days were the most unforgettable days we will ever have as a family. I will forever be grateful to the Make-A-Wish foundation and all of their partners and donors for those six precious days they gave our family.

October 23, 2014—Six Years Old

We headed to Chicago that morning to see his new orthopedic surgeon to discuss Bracey's future. I was feeling hopeful for Bracey's future. I hadn't heard any results from his most recent tests, and I was anxious to get them.

His doctor came in and went over the MRI, EKG, and ultrasounds. He said it looked as if Bracey's spinal cord was twisted around the hemivertebrae. I asked him what that meant, and he said it makes for a more sensitive transplant of the rods. They would have to be very careful and have steady hands as to not nick the spinal cord. One wrong movement, and Bracey could be paralyzed. I asked him what our options were at that point.

He discussed the two different type of rods that could be used. One was very common and had been around for many years, which was the VEPTR growing rod. The other option was MAGEC growing rods. They both had different pros and cons for Bracey's condition. Also, our doctor was not as familiar with the MAGEC rods and had never used them. He and a group of doctors would be meeting in the days to follow to discuss Bracey's case.

We went home, and research began all over again: VEPTR versus MAGEC. For the next few months, I learned everything I absolutely could about these two different growing rods. I knew which doctors and hospitals in the United States were the best with these rods. I knew what type of metal they were, who manufactured them, how they worked, the longevity of them, the infection rates, what each transplant entailed, how long each lasted until they needed to be replaced, and what the replacement surgery was like. I read the success stories and the horror stories. I craved knowledge about these rods. One of these types of rods was going to change my son's life. I needed to be as informed as I possibly could.

December 17, 2014—Six Years Old

Bracey had another respiratory infection. It came on overnight. With Christmas quickly approaching, I did not want to chance him getting hospitalized. I had called his pulmonologist, and she said she could see him. So, we headed down to Indy. I didn't think he needed to be admitted. I felt we caught it before it had really settled in his chest. When we got to her office, he had a fever, and his oxygen was resting at 90 percent.

She sent us down to the ER to have some tests, an x-ray, and to get a double breathing treatment, which had to be done while hooked up to the monitors. After four hours in the ER, Bracey was doing much better. He had taken a double breathing treatment, which really helped him. His oxygen was up to 96 percent. His x-ray did confirm pneumonia, and blood tests confirmed influenza A. I felt comfortable taking him home and continuing his treatments and vest therapy there. I prayed this wasn't the beginning of a long winter for our little guy.

February 2015—Seven Years Old

We made it seven weeks without Bracey getting sick! This was pretty impressive considering it was winter season. However, on February 15, 2015, Bracey began to throw up. He was coughing and throwing up every twenty minutes. After twenty-four hours of continuously throwing up, we decided to take to him to our local ER. He was unable to walk. His calves looked like little rocks. His feet were beginning to curve in. I knew this scenario all too well. Bracey was dehydrated and needed an IV. The nurse got his IV in, and Bracey didn't even flinch. He sat there and just watched her. He was so impressive. She drew blood and started him on saline.

A little while later, the ER doctor came in and said his numbers showed he was very dehydrated. They had given him some medicine through the IV to help with the nausea. He didn't throw up again after that medication was given. After about four hours in the ER, he was well on his way to feeling better. That anti-nausea medication was amazing. Within two days, he was back to being my Bracey!

A few months had gone by since we last saw the orthopedic surgeon doctor in Chicago. I felt so uneasy. I was interested in what the doctor had to say, but after my intensive research, I did not have a clear decision.

We did another set of x-rays that morning, and the doctor came in and said it looked as though his curvature was eleven to thirteen degrees more than his latest x-rays that were back in the fall.

The doctor was strongly suggesting VETPR rods. The surgery would be about five hours, and he would have about a week of recovery in the hospital. The doctor would also separate Bracey's fused ribs at that time. The doctor agreed this surgery should allow his lung to expand.

This specialized ortho hospital did not have an actual pulmonary team, but they would be in communication with Bracey's pulmonologist in Indy. We left his office believing Bracey would be getting scheduled for this surgery quite soon, but I had an unpeaceful feeling about all of it.

On the drive home, I asked Bracey, like I always do, if he understood everything the doctor was talking about or if he had any questions. He said, "Mommy, I just want to feel better." As tears swelled up in my eyes, I assured him we were working on making sure he got the best and safest treatment possible to help heal his body.

As the next few days went by, I got very little sleep. I tossed and turned. Praying to God. Seeking wisdom from our pulmonologist. Seeking wisdom from other families. Why couldn't I get peace about this? Were my emotions about putting Bracey through another major surgery clouding my judgment? This surgery would be life-changing for Bracey. It was something we had been working toward for two years! Why was I so hesitant? I should be so happy for Bracey. I should feel hopeful for his future, yet I felt so uncertain.

One of the most important things in my life is Bracey's health. I had spent the last seven years fighting for Bracey—being his voice. And here it was, a chance to give Bracey the life he deserved. A life without multiple hospitalizations a year. A life without oxygen machines. A life where he could run and kick a ball and not have to take a rest because he couldn't breathe. A life with two functioning lungs. This was the life I had dreamed of for Bracey for seven years.

"So, God, why don't I have peace? Bracey is in Your hands, God, but please help us make the best decision."

To our family and friends, it seemed like a no-brainer. I had been anxious about every surgery and hospitalization Bracey had, but I had always had peace about them. This feeling was very different, and it continued to weigh on me.

I called to speak with his pulmonologist. I explained the surgery, recovery, and my feelings toward it all. She had some of the same concerns—namely, the fact they didn't have a pulmonary care team. Bracey's lung care was very fragile, and it was very important to me he had pulmonary care while in the hospital. I assured her I would keep her posted on what we decided.

Meanwhile, when I was doing my intensive research a few months back, I had come across a certain hospital in Philadelphia. Even as we moved toward our team in Chicago, this hospital remained in the back of my mind. They had a team of doctors that specialized in congenital scoliosis and VEPTR growing rods.

But Philadelphia was more than seven hundred miles away from us. We could never go there, I thought. This hospital, and a very specific doctor there, kept coming back to my mind. I felt God tugging at me to seek them out.

The evening of March 2, 2015, just four days after our visit to Chicago, I sat down with Torrey and asked him his thoughts on the surgery in Chicago. He mentioned his reservations about the pulmonary care as well. He wasn't 100 percent at peace with the surgery being in Chicago either. We both agreed the doctors, nurses, and facilities there were wonderful, but they just weren't for Bracey at this time. I asked him about looking into another option.

We both knew this would mean delaying the surgery. Bracey's curve was only getting worse, and so were the continued lung infections. We talked with Bracey and explained we didn't feel comfortable with him having his back surgery in Chicago but assured him we were going to find the best care for him.

I told him there was a really big hospital in Philadelphia we would like to try to see. I told him it was near the ocean and maybe someday we would get to go see the ocean. He, like always, just smiled and said, "Okay, Mommy."

That evening, I got on the phone with a friend of mine whose child had the VEPTR growing rods, and they were going to Philadelphia as well. We talked for almost forty-five minutes as she helped answer a lot of questions and gave some great insight and encouragement about pursuing care at the hospital in Philadelphia. She gave me some contact information for a nurse in Philadelphia.

March 8, 2015—Seven Years Old

I made the initial contact to a nurse in Philadelphia. She was very quick to respond, and I could tell she would be my main advocate as we began this journey. She emailed me a list of things she and the doctor needed to prepare an initial review of Bracey's case. Within two weeks, I had sent off every last piece of information I had on Bracey. Medical charts/history, all of his doctors, every scan, scope, ultrasound, EKG, x-ray, surgery, and medications were on their way across the country.

I received a call on May 4, 2015, from Philadelphia. The doctor had reviewed all of Bracey's information and wanted to meet with Bracey in the doctor's clinic in Philadelphia. We were so excited! Over the next two weeks, I worked almost daily, talking with the insurance and Bracey's primary care physician. We needed a referral and authorization codes.

About four weeks later, the clinic in Philadelphia contacted me to let me know they still did not have everything they needed from our PCP, but they wanted to go ahead and get Bracey on the schedule before it filled up.

We were scheduled to be in Philadelphia the week of July 6. It would be a long few days of seeing multiple doctors, having multiple tests, and a three-dimensional MRI, for which he would need to be sedated. Having that date on my calendar felt like a huge weight had been taken off of my shoulders. I had such a calming peace about it. I could not wait to see this state-of-the-art hospital. I could not wait to show the kids the ocean. Everything was falling into place.

June 3, 2015—Seven Years Old

Bracey woke up in the night coughing, and I just knew. I called his pulmonologist the next morning, and they got him in that day. I packed our just-in-case bag and headed to Indy. His doctor said Bracey had pneumonia. I pleaded with her to let us go home. She knew I would watch over him closely and follow our routine of every-four-hour treatments day and night. She ordered him a steroid and an antibiotic. I thanked her for letting us go home. Well, the next day, Bracey was worse. His oxygen was low, and he needed a double treatment. Double treatments did Bracey a world of wonders, but he had to be monitored during them because his heart rate could skyrocket during and after the treatment. Off to the local ER we went. I explained to them what he needed. They usually only look at me like I'm crazy for a second, and then they realize this is not my first experience. After a couple of hours, Bracey was bouncing back and feeling much better. We went home and continued our healing regimen.

On June 17, 2015, I heard from our nurse in Philadelphia. They were still having trouble getting authorization codes. I had been talking with our PCP for weeks, and I was exhausted. I asked Torrey if he could please call them and explain the importance of this information, as we were at risk of having to reschedule our appointments.

He called, and they assured him they were working on it. Unfortunately, in a case like this, my pulmonologist could not be the referral, nor could she get the authorization codes they needed. I felt as if Bracey's future rested on getting the authorization codes from the PCP. I felt ignorant dealing with insurance. I did not understand all of the ins and outs and the terminology the insurance company used. It was one of my absolute least favorite parts of Bracey's medical trials, yet it held such power over my son's future.

A few short days later, Bracey was sick again. I knew he needed medical help. I packed our bags, called our pulmonologist, and headed down to the ER in Indy. The ER was expecting us and had a room on the floor ready for us when we got there. Bracey's oxygen level was low. They put him on oxygen immediately and started a double breathing treatment. Even with the oxygen, he was working hard to breathe. They were talking about admitting him to the PICU floor. I obviously wanted them to do what they felt was best; I trusted them, but I also shared with them my concern about being on the PICU floor at such a crucial time.

We were just days away from going to Philadelphia, and if Bracey was put on the PICU floor, that would mean a longer stay at the hospital. Selfishly, I wanted him on the regular floor. His team of doctors finally decided to keep him on the main floor. And although that should have helped me feel relieved, it somehow didn't.

Bracey fought hard all night. His oxygen levels were all over the place. It would read down in the low eighties. I jostled him and pounded on his back to make him cough, and his oxygen would come back up to the nineties. Every time that oxygen alarm went off, my heart sank. I jumped up and silenced it. I hated that alarm. That alarm was just an annoying sound pushing us further and further away from being able to go to Philadelphia.

I was running on thirty-eight hours with no sleep, and my emotions and exhausted state of mind were getting the best of me. Bracey continued like this until the next afternoon. On June 30, 2015, just five days before we were supposed to leave for Philadelphia, Bracey started feeling better. He woke up from a short nap and asked to eat. He got out of his bed and sat on our couch. I ordered him a plate of food and put a movie on for him. It was so good to see him awake, eating, and talking.

His pulmonologist came in later that afternoon and sat on the couch with us. She said Bracey sounded better. She still heard very little to no air movement in his left lung though. She moved him to every-three-hour increments for breathing treatments. Then she looked me in the eye and said she did not feel it would be wise for us to take Bracey to Philadelphia this week. He needed to be put to sleep for some of his tests, and his body was not ready for that yet. As tears streamed down my face, I told her I had known she would say that. I told her I felt like we'd come so far and were so close to getting him the help he needed.

She wrapped her arms around me and said she knew this was hard, but Bracey had an amazing family, and we had always put his best interests first. It was not safe to put Bracey under anesthesia for a few more weeks. His body needed time to heal from this infection. I knew she was right. She always helped me see things clearly when my thoughts and emotions clouded my decisions.

July 2, 2015—Seven Years Old

After fighting for Bracey and trying to pretend he wasn't *that* sick, I came to the realization that putting our trip across the country on hold was the best thing for him. I made the tough call to Philadelphia to tell them he was in the hospital, and although he would probably be going home, he wasn't well enough to make the trip to Philadelphia and go through the tests. They absolutely understood and said we would talk about getting back on the schedule after the holiday.

We were discharged that day, but Bracey had to go home on oxygen. Although Torrey and I were very disappointed to not be going to Philadelphia right then, it was wonderful to be a family again after the tiresome hospital stay. Bracey was doing well with his treatments every four hours, but he still needed the oxygen at night.

We went to my parents' house for the July 4 holiday weekend and had the oxygen delivered there. Bracey continued to need oxygen at night for the next couple of days.

The day after we were released from the hospital, we were having lunch, and Bracey started choking. So as to not frighten his cousins, I calmly and quickly took him to the bathroom, where I gave him the Heimlich. The larger piece of food came out, and he said he still had some stuck in there. We were in the bathroom, and as he leaned over the toilet, I rubbed his back to keep him calm as the other pieces worked themselves up. It took almost ten minutes, but little by little, the small pieces of food worked their way out of Bracey's esophagus. He wasn't scared or upset. This was his life. It was almost routine for him.

He knew when he needed to take a drink to help push the food down. He knew when the food wasn't going to go down. He knew to remain calm no matter how scary it was. He was accustomed to this part of life.

Anger began to build up in my heart. I was so tired of seeing my little guy sick. He shouldn't have to be accustomed to choking. He shouldn't have to go through surgery after surgery, doctor appointment after doctor appointment, hospitalization after hospitalization, x-ray after x-ray, medication after medication, infection after infection, choking fit after choking fit, cough after cough, and breathing treatment after breathing treatment! The list went on and on. I saw little boys and girls out playing, running, and kicking balls, while my little guy stood on the sideline because his chest was tight and he couldn't breathe. I knew all he wanted to do was kick that ball, make that goal, play that game, climb that playset, run in that field … yet I watched him standing on the sidelines.

He was not angry. He was not pouting. He was not upset or crying. He was excited and cheered for his friends, his teammates. He was all smiles and encouraged them to keep going. *If Bracey can find joy, then why can't I?* I asked God to help me see Bracey's life through Bracey's eyes. He was full of joy and compassion, yet *he* was the one with the physical limitations. I wanted to stop feeling sorry for myself and for Bracey. He didn't feel sorry for himself. He didn't see himself as different. He continued to love life and make the best out of what he could do. He did not use

126

his limitations as an excuse to not try things. He continued to be determined to do the best he could at everything he did.

"Lord, help me. Please take this selfish, pity-party heart away. Thank You for allowing Bracey to teach me more about compassion and determination. Help me to constantly be trusting in You and turning my eyes toward You. Bracey truly is in Your hands. Thank You for reminding me of that."

August 2015—Seven Years Old

After finally getting Bracey back to his normal baseline health, we were ready to reschedule our trip to Philadelphia. I emailed our liaison nurse and told her he was doing much better and we would like to get our appointments rescheduled. About a week later, we got a tough call. Bracey's insurance was not budging and would not approve our appointments anymore. *What? How could this be?* We had been set to go in July, and there hadn't seemed to be any problems then.

His insurance company had agreed to approve Bracey seeing the doctor for a consultation but would not approve any tests, procedures, or surgeries. I didn't understand all of this. Even though I had dealt with insurance a lot, exponentially more since Bracey's birth, it still confused me. Insurance companies are constantly changing their laws, restrictions, plans, and policies. *What should we do now?* We had worked so hard for this. This was the hospital I felt was the perfect place for us. None of this made sense to me. After hours of tears and overwhelming disappointment, I found peace knowing God had something else in store for us.

Torrey spoke with the insurance company, and they gave us two hospitals that would be approved for Bracey. One hospital was in Memphis, Tennessee, and the other one was in Cincinnati, Ohio. Both of these hospitals had come up during the extensive research I had done. I had researched two specific doctors that did VEPTR growing rods in each location. Now I needed to do more intensive research on each hospital and doctor for Torrey and I to determine which one would be best for Bracey.

I began researching. I called my friend who had been so helpful a few months back. She offered additional information on both hospitals. I spoke with our pulmonologist, and she was able to give insightful information as well. I read blogs of personal experiences with both doctors. I revisited my study of VEPTR versus MAGEC growing rods. It was obvious to me one of these two doctors and hospitals was going to be our future.

In September 2015, we decided it would be wise for Bracey to have his G-tube placed again. With back surgery looming in the near future and the choking episodes he continued to experience, we, along with the doctors, felt it would be best for Bracey to have a second way for him to get nutrients. I had peace about this, as I knew Bracey would benefit from this procedure. The doctor hoped she would be able to use the same tract his previous G-tube was in, but she wouldn't be sure until surgery. We prayed Bracey would be able to use the same tract. If that was possible, it meant very little recovery time, and he wouldn't need an additional surgery to move from the temporary tube to the main Minnie button. His pulmonologist wanted him to get a sleep study done before the surgery, and while Bracey was still healthy, this was the best time for it.

September 19, 2015—Seven Years Old

Bracey had a sleep study done. Sleep studies are brutal. Our hospital tries to make it as much like home as possible, except for the wires all over your head and chest. The room was cozy. It looked just like a bedroom would. They even had a fan for fan lovers like us. Once we got there and settled in, the technician came in and hooked Bracey up. This process took about an hour. Then it was time to sleep. It took Bracey a while to fall asleep that night. I spent an hour telling him a story, singing him some songs, and praying. Finally, he dozed off to sleep. I am sure the technicians were very happy when he finally fell asleep. Bracey did pretty well. He slept for almost five hours, which was impressive, considering he was hooked up to all kinds of wires and he wasn't supposed to roll over. That was tough for a tummy sleeper.

When he woke up, our technician came in and cleaned him up and said we could go. So, at five o'clock on a Saturday morning, we headed back home. His sleep study showed a normal sleep pattern and minor snoring. With a good report of the sleep study, we were ready to schedule the G-tube placement.

October 15, 2015—Seven Years Old

The mornings of surgeries were rough on me. I was always anxious on surgery day. I knew we had made the right decision to have Bracey's G-tube placed back in, but we did not really know what the immediate outcome of this surgery would entail. Would Bracey wake up with a button or with a temporary tube that required additional surgery to replace that with the permanent button? I had been praying from the day we scheduled this surgery for the doctor to be able to use the previous tract. One less surgery would be fantastic. Not only that, but Bracey wouldn't have any incisions, and we wouldn't have to mess with that annoying temporary tube (Malecot tube). Soon the nurse came, and Bracey happily walked back to the OR with her as we stopped at that dreaded red line.

After what seemed like a very short hour, our doctor came out with a huge smile on her face. I knew what that smile meant. She was able to use the previous tract. That was fantastic news! Bracey was breathing very well. He needed to stay in the hospital for the next twenty-four hours to make sure the button was draining properly, which would verify the button was in place and his tract was working well.

That next afternoon, Bracey was doing great, and the tract looked beautiful. We started feeding through the tract. He was a little tender, but everything looked great. The doctor wrote up discharge papers, and another successful surgery was in the books.

By late October, Torrey and I had decided on an orthopedic doctor and hospital for Bracey's back journey. We had decided to go with the doctor and hospital in Memphis, Tennessee. I contacted the doctor and nurses there. The doctor and I began emailing. He answered so many questions about what to expect for our initial visit. He was extremely helpful and very personable. We scheduled our initial visit for December 15.

I was anxious. I could not wait to meet this doctor and his staff. I was anxious to see the hospital. But, mostly, I was ready to move forward to get Bracey the help he needed.

December 15, 2015—Seven Years Old

We had our vehicle packed up, and our little family of four began our six-hundred-mile trip down to Memphis, Tennessee. The hospital had a house near it for families to stay in, and they had reserved a room for our family. Those eight hours seemed to go by quickly. It really was a straight shot from our house to Memphis.

Driving over the Mississippi River into Memphis was breathtaking. It was such a beautiful bridge. To the left was what quickly became one of our favorite places to visit while in Memphis, the Bass Pro Shop Pyramid. We turned off the interstate and onto the side street, where we saw the hospital. It was huge and beautiful! There was such excitement in our little car that day. That was our hospital. That was where Bracey's life was going to change. That was where we were going to begin new memories and a new future.

We pulled into the gated parking lot adjacent to the huge house where we were staying. The parking lot was landscaped beautifully. As we walked into that huge home, we were instantly greeted with smiles and helpful staff. There was a warm, cozy fireplace. There were lots of sitting areas for my family to enjoy while I checked us in. The children were given little gift bags filled with goodies ranging from gummy bears to coloring books. They took us on a tour of the house. Every family had their own mini-fridge that stayed locked. That was super helpful since some of Bracey's medication required refrigeration.

On the main floor, there were multiple kitchens for the families to use, with many shareable foods and pantry items. There was a large eating area and a large living area with movies available. On the room floors, there were washers and dryers for the families to use. The house even provided laundry detergent! There were foosball tables, couches, and televisions. My kids were in awe of the size of the house and everything it had to offer. As we walked to our guest room, the kids were jumping and running with excitement. We tried to calm and quiet them since others may have been sleeping.

We opened the bedroom door, and our faces just lit up. It was so airy and refreshing. Everything sparkled. The hardwood floors shined. There were two beds and a television in the main room, and then off the main room was a living area with two comfy swivel chairs and a large window bench that could be turned into another bed. Off of the living area was the extra-large bathroom with a double vanity. Everything smelled, looked, and felt clean. It was such a blessing to have a beautiful place we could return to and rest in after a long day at the hospital.

December 16, 2015—Seven Years Old

The initial visit with the orthopedic surgeon could not have gone better. Upon checking in, they sent Bracey for an x-ray. This wasn't a normal x-ray. It used a machine called an EOS imaging system. EOS captures head-to-toe images in a standing position. The low-dose digital images allow for 3-D bone modeling. EOS emits about 10 percent of the radiation of a traditional CT scan. It took only about thirty seconds to scan his entire body. It was amazing to see every single detail of his spine and ribs. You could clearly see every hemivertebra, his fused ribs, and the curve of his spine. It was incredible. I had never seen his insides so clearly before.

Shortly after, the doctor walked in. As soon as he opened the door, his smile lit up our room. He was so friendly. He sat down beside Bracey right away and started talking to him. I was amazed. I was in awe of how personable he was and how he sat down next to Bracey and just started talking to him as if Bracey was his own son. He asked Bracey all about his school, hobbies, favorite foods, favorite places to visit, and more. It was obvious this doctor loved children and treated them as his own and not as a no-name textbook patient. He even included Brynn, our daughter, in his conversation.

After about fifteen minutes, he asked Bracey if it would be okay for him to speak with his mom and dad for a bit. I am sure I looked like a cheesy goof as I sat in awe, grinning from ear to ear.

The doctor said he had looked over Bracey's history and reviewed the scan he just had. He estimated Bracey's spinal curve to be between seventy and seventy-five degrees. I expressed my concerns about Bracey's lungs and how I was hesitant to do anything without the consent of our pulmonologist. I expressed to him how important it was to me he spoke with our pulmonologist before any surgeries. He assured me he would.

Then we went on to talk about treatment. He was in strong agreement that surgery would most definitely improve Bracey's lung function. We discussed the two options for his surgery, one being the VEPTR rods and the other being the MAGEC rods. I told him, after a lot of research, we were very interested in the MAGEC rods.

We felt, with Bracey's lung condition, VEPTR rods would not be preferred. They required multiple surgeries to lengthen the rods every six months. MAGEC rods were lengthened with a remote control, and it was done in the clinic. It was noninvasive, and all adjustments were done externally. There were no additional surgeries involved with the lengthening procedures. That meant a much lower risk of infection, a lot less anxiety for Bracey, and zero recovery time. We could literally get his rods lengthened and walk out of the office within minutes.

The doctor agreed, given Bracey's medical history, the MAGEC rods would be the way to go. He could not guarantee Bracey could get the MAGEC growing rods until he was in surgery with him, but everything was pointing in that direction.

He would have VEPTR rods on standby in case Bracey's spine was not a good candidate for MAGEC rods. He needed to have a small section of straight spine for the magnetic part of the hardware. The doctor understood the importance of Bracey not having surgery in the winter time if at all possible. He agreed we could wait until spring or summer. He explained he was not one to rush into spinal surgeries. He wanted time to study the 3-D model they would be making of Bracey's spine and rib cavity. He scheduled for us to come back in three months to get a 3-D CT scan so they could build the model.

We left Memphis feeling very optimistic about Bracey's future. Torrey and I both had such peace about finally finding *the perfect doctor for Bracey*. We thanked God for allowing the many hiccups along the way that led us to Memphis.

March 1, 2016—Eight Years Old

January and February went by quickly. Bracey struggled daily with his coughing. We had such a tough time getting it under control. It wasn't affecting his appetite or demeanor, so he continued to go to school. The last week in February, I could tell his cough was more persistent. His choking episodes were increasing. His oxygen levels were in the low nineties during the day. I made an appointment with his pulmonologist.

I headed down to Indy with Bracey. His pulmonologist was able to see him right away. She put him on another steroid and added an additional breathing medication to his nebulizer. I was confident that after just a few hours of being on the new meds, Bracey would begin to bounce back. That evening, his cough turned from junky to tight. He wasn't coughing anything up, and he said his chest hurt. I called the pulmonologist, and she put him on an antibiotic to help cover his lungs. I was still hopeful he would be able to recover at home.

Night came, though, and Bracey was unable to sleep due to the constant coughing. I made him a bed on the couch, where he could sleep sitting up. I monitored his oxygen levels closely and realized they were not staying in the nineties. They would dip into the mideighties and would not come back up unless I forced Bracey to cough. I knew he needed more help than I could offer him at home. So, the next morning, we headed back down the 150 miles to Indy. The doctor had asked me to go straight to the ER; she would let them know we were coming.

We were about an hour down the interstate when I heard some rumbling. I knew we were on a loud section of the road, so I didn't pay any attention to it. Seconds later, I saw my entire tire flying off behind me. I was in the left-hand lane passing a semitruck. I quickly moved over to the shoulder and saw my rear tire was completely gone.

I got my spare out of the trunk and the tire jack tools. I had no clue what to do with them, so I just prayed God would send someone to our rescue. I needed to get Bracey down to his pulmonologist in Indy, and I was still about two hours away. He would need a breathing treatment soon.

In my rearview mirror, I saw a city truck with three men in it. They pulled behind me and asked if they could help me. I was so relieved. They told me to stay in the car, and they would put my spare on for me. Within ten minutes, they had my spare tire on and had given me directions to the nearest tire shop. It was quite the adventure. While at the tire shop, I was able to give Bracey a breathing treatment. Within an hour, we were on our way.

We finally arrived at the hospital, and his doctor immediately gave Bracey a breathing treatment. It was a double treatment, which took about forty-five minutes. During the treatment, his oxygen level went up to ninety-three. After the treatment, he had a couple chest x-rays done. His doctor came in and reported Bracey had bilateral pneumonia. His oxygen level had stayed in the low to midnineties even hours after his treatment. His doctor wanted us to stay through another treatment. If his oxygen levels stayed in the nineties, she would let us go home. Four more hours went by, and the respiratory therapist came in to give him another treatment. His oxygen remained constant at ninety-four. After the treatment, he had some really good coughs and didn't sound tight anymore. I knew he was going to be okay, and I was comfortable taking him home. By March 6, 2016, Bracey was back to himself. He was happy, eating, and feeling much better. He still had a cough, but it was controlled.

March 15, 2016—Eight Years Old

It was time for another trip to Memphis. We were excited to see our doctor again and gain more information about Bracey's back surgery. The four of us got to Memphis the day before our appointments. Memphis is such a cool city. There is so much to do and see. It's large, but it doesn't feel like a large city. That evening, we went to what quickly became our favorite BBQ joint and, of course, the Bass Pro Shop. If you haven't been to Memphis Bass Pro Shop, I highly recommend it!

The next morning, we headed over to the clinic. Bracey had another EOS (x-ray) of his spine. I was still amazed and impressed by this type of x-ray. It's so precise and low radiation. Our doctor walked in and again greeted us with his amazing smile. He spent time talking to both Bracey and Brynn, asking all sorts of questions. My six-year-old, Brynn, was very happy to answer them, and she had a bunch of questions for him. She has always been curious about Bracey's medical condition, and she loves watching doctors work with him. The doctor was very thorough, and we all agreed it was time to schedule his surgery. We wanted a summer surgery so Bracey would have time to recover before school started.

The doctor agreed we could make that happen. He wanted Bracey to be followed by one of the pulmonologists in Memphis, and he wanted to get a 3-D cat scan of Bracey's spine. He needed all of this by May so his team could build an exact 3-D model of Bracey's back, which the doctor would study prior to surgery. He was still hopeful Bracey would be able to receive the MAGEC growing rods. We left Memphis again, feeling encouraged and at such peace about Bracey's future.

God has definitely had His hand in every aspect of Bracey's life. The family who first told me about this doctor was a family

I knew from high school, whose son had some similar medical issues. I have no doubt God had this plan for Bracey years before his birth.

It's so awesome how God places us exactly where we need to be. We may not understand in the moment, and we may not like it, but He has a reason for our lives. I thank God daily that He is my Lord. What an awesome, all-knowing, and powerful God I get to serve!

April 15, 2016—Eight Years Old

Bracey's cough never completely went away. A few days before April 15, I could tell his cough was increasing and getting tight. He was coughing through the night and had developed a low-grade fever. I called his pulmonologist and told her I thought we should go straight to the ER. All of his signs pointed to pneumonia, and with the weekend ahead of us, I didn't want to chance him getting worse.

So, that morning, I packed an overnight bag, just in case, and I headed down to Indy. Bracey had to get better and stay better for just a couple of months. We had a very busy next few months scheduled, preparing for the surgery. We needed to go back down to Memphis to meet the pulmonary team down there, he still needed to get his CT scan completed, and we needed him well enough to complete these things before the big day.

We got to the ER at ten thirty in the morning. His x-ray showed pneumonia, as I had expected, and the doctor wanted to admit him. By noon, we were in our hospital room. They started him on breathing treatments every two hours. They began an oral steroid and an antibiotic to help cover his lungs. It was a long, tiring day.

Torrey and Brynn came down after he got off from work. It was always a relief to see them. My parents came and spent a little bit of time with us and took Brynn back home with them. Torrey stayed with me and Bracey. Bracey's oxygen level dropped into the eighties that night. I knew the doctor would never let him leave the hospital if he wasn't staying in the nineties.

The following afternoon, Bracey was acting better. He still had a low-grade fever, so we could not visit the playroom. Instead, we spent the day watching movies, playing games, and building Legos. The doctors agreed to decrease his treatments to every three hours. This allowed more resting time in between treatments. It was tough, especially during the night, to be doing treatments every two hours.

Bracey had a good night. His oxygen level stayed around ninety-four, and his fever was finally gone. I knew he was on the mend.

The next morning, the doctor agreed to move him to every-four-hour treatments. I knew if Bracey could go four hours in between treatments without needing one, he could go home.

Early that afternoon, the doctor came in and said Bracey was doing better and asked if I felt comfortable taking him home. Yes, I was definitely comfortable with that. We packed up our things, met up with my parents to get Brynn, and back home we went. I kept Bracey home from school one more day to make sure he was getting the rest and the treatments he needed. He was soon back to his baseline, and we were ready to prepare for his back surgery.

April 27, 2016—Eight Years Old

Our orthopedic doctor's scheduler called and gave us a surgery date as well as two dates we needed to come to Memphis, prior to surgery, for some tests. Our surgery was officially scheduled for July 1, 2016!

May 22, 2016—Eight Years Old

It was time to head back down to Memphis to get the CT scan and meet the pulmonary team who would be with Bracey. We were also scheduled to get a tour of the hospital and meet with the anesthesiologist who would be with Bracey the day of his surgery. We were especially excited about this visit because we were told the FedEx House, the house we stayed at before, was full, but they were putting us up at a very nice hotel just down the street. The best part was that this hotel had an indoor pool. The kids had a blast. They swam for a bit, and then we went to our favorite BBQ place, visited the Bass Pro Shop, and then explored the large hotel. It was graduation season, and there was a large graduation ceremony going on. We went up to the top floor and were able to look over the Mississippi River. It was beautiful. It was near evening, and the bridge had the lights on, and the Bass Pro Shop pyramid was lit up as well. The city looked so beautiful that evening. We loved being at the FedEx House, but this was a fun evening for our family.

The next morning, we took Bracey over for the CT scan. He did great and was able to lie so still that they did not have to sedate him. After his scan, a child life specialist gave us a tour of the hospital. The lady was amazing with Bracey. She talked to him and asked him and Brynn all kinds of questions while we walked around.

She took us to a pre-op room and explained what the morning of his surgery would look like. She showed him pictures of nurses and doctors in gowns and masks. He was very familiar with that picture. She showed him a picture of what an operating room looked like. He was impressed, and Brynn had so many questions. She is quite intrigued with medicine. The specialist walked us through the tunnel of gifts. This tunnel is for every patient. They get to pick out a toy before heading into the operating room. Then she let us look through the window of an operating room.

She explained they have a program at their hospital that allows one parent to go into the operating room with their child as he falls asleep if the parent would like. I was so ecstatic about this program and most definitely wanted to do it. I am not a fan of the red line, and my heart was jumping with joy knowing I didn't have to hand my baby off to a stranger. I could hold his hands and talk to him while he peacefully fell asleep.

Although Bracey had proved to be quite the trooper with countless surgeries under his belt, I could be with him until he fell asleep. That was very soothing to this mama's soul. The idea of Bracey going into surgery as relaxed and comfortable as possible was a huge comfort to both the parents and the child. Allowing the child to have peace and having Mom's face be the last face he sees before falling asleep is reassuring. I think every single children's hospital should adopt this program.

After the tour, we met with the anesthesiologist who would be with Bracey during and after the surgery. He immediately made a connection with Bracey. He understood the struggles Bracey had in the past and was very patient with us as we explained to him our concerns. We knew this surgery would be long and Bracey would need to be intubated. Our main concern was how quickly he would be able to have the breathing tube removed. The doctor made all kinds of notes and was very aware of Bracey's lung issues. He said he would stay with Bracey until he was extubated. We thanked him and knew we were in good hands.

Next, we headed over to the pulmonary clinic to meet the team that would be managing Bracey's lung function during his stay. The doctor was very knowledgeable of Bracey's condition. She wanted Bracey to start using a medical instrument called the Acapella device. It is a device that, when breathed into, forces him to cough to keep his airways cleared. After the surgery, Bracey would not be able to use his smart vest, which vibrated his lungs to help clear them, so this would do a similar thing.

The pulmonary doctor also wanted a sleep study. As I said before, Bracey and I hate sleep studies. They expected Bracey to sleep through the night while hooked up to a bunch of little wires all over his head, chest, and face. And then they tell you not to roll over. How can they get an accurate account of his sleep patterns if he's not allowed to sleep like he would at home? Nevertheless, we did as they asked and scheduled the sleep study. We were confident in this pulmonary team and knew they would take good care of Bracey.

As we headed home that evening, we were actually excited for his surgery. It was the first time in Bracey's life we were excited about a surgery. We knew without a shadow of a doubt that we were in the best place for Bracey. It had been a long road to get here, but we thanked God for all of the bumps in the road. At the time, those bumps seemed so discouraging.

We knew now that God had a plan and wanted to lead us to Memphis.

June 6, 2016—Eight Years Old

We made one last trip to Memphis before the big day. One more visit to see his doctor and then the dreaded sleep study. We had a few extra days, so we decided to head down by way of St. Louis, Missouri. The kids had never been to St. Louis, and we wanted to do something special with them before the big day. Just as we hoped, they were in awe of the arch. We drove by the arch on the way to the hotel.

The kids were so excited. They couldn't wait to go up in it. We stayed at this sweet hotel. It had an indoor pool for the kids to play in. The next morning, we took a tour of the arch and went up to the top. What an experience that was! The kids and Torrey loved it. They had so much fun, and I loved seeing their smiles. I have a fear of heights and tight spaces, so I did not enjoy going up, but I did enjoy watching the excitement on their faces. They had such joy and amazement in their eyes.

We said goodbye to St. Louis and continued our little trip down to Memphis. Bracey was scheduled for the sleep study that evening. We also visited our favorite BBQ place and the Bass Pro Shop on our way to the appointment.

Torrey and Brynn dropped Bracey and me off at the hospital. We were taken to our room, and shortly thereafter, the technician had Bracey hooked up. She turned the lights off, and Bracey was supposed to fall asleep. He had a tough time falling asleep. I sang a bit to him and told him a story. He finally seemed be getting sleepy, so we prayed, and I kissed him goodnight.

I lay on the little couch beside him. It was a terrible night's rest. At four o'clock in the morning, Bracey woke up and had to go to the bathroom. I knew there was no way he would fall back to sleep. The technician came in and unhooked him. He went to the bathroom, and then she hooked him back up. She asked if he could try to fall back to sleep. I said we would try, but it was doubtful. An hour went by, and he was obviously not going to fall back to sleep. They were able to get four hours of the sleep study. The tech came back in and unhooked him. We were free to leave. I called Torrey, and he and Brynn came to pick us up, and we headed back home to Indiana. Just a few more weeks until Bracey's big surgery day!

June 29, 2016—Eight Years Old

This was the day we headed down south to begin Bracey's new journey. It had been years of searching and researching to get to this point. It had also been years of pneumonia, hospitalizations, low oxygen levels, fevers, doctor visits, antibiotics, steroids, choking episodes, poor lung function, x-rays, endless breathing treatments, missed school, and cancelled activities. Those days were about to be a thing of the past. I knew this surgery would tremendously change Bracey's life. I knew his lung function would improve greatly. Bracey was about to be given the opportunity to become a healthier little boy. He would still have a long road of orthopedic appointments and multiple back surgeries, but I knew his lung health would be better for it. And breathing was the most important thing.

I experienced so many mixed emotions during this time. We decided it would be best if Brynn did not come with us right away. And even though it was the best choice, it was tough to leave her behind. We left her in Southern Indiana with her Aunt Tenisha, Uncle Jason, and cousins, who I knew would spoil her. I knew she would have a blast. She was in good hands, and they would bring her to see us a few days after the surgery. We kissed her goodbye and continued on down to Memphis.

June 30, 2016—Eight Years Old

It was the day before surgery. We spent a few hours with pre-op appointments and met with the anesthesiologist again. He was still fabulous, and I knew Bracey would be in good hands. Bracey had blood work done and one last x-ray, and we learned the very specific instructions on how to bathe Bracey before his surgery.

That afternoon, both Torrey's and my parents came into town. We took them to our favorite BBQ place and to the Bass Pro Shop. Bracey loved having all his grandparents there. They were such a great distraction to us all.

As always, I did not sleep well that night before surgery. I knew we were doing exactly what Bracey needed. This was what we had prayed for, for so long. However, it is still so emotional to put your child's life in someone else's hands.

Having to kiss him and tell him "sweet dreams" would be tough. I hated knowing he would wake up and be confused from the medication. I hated knowing he would have to endure pain. I hated that it couldn't be me enduring this pain for him. Bracey knew what to expect. Part of me felt that was wonderful, and the rest of me found it heartbreaking. I loved being able to talk with him about it, but it broke my heart when he asked how much pain he would be in. I had a tough time answering that question. I looked at my sweet boy's face and said, "You know what, buddy, you may be in some discomfort for a few days, but all you have to do is tell me or Daddy, and we will make sure you get medicine to help take the discomfort away."

July 1, 2016—Surgery Day

We had to be at the hospital by six o'clock in the morning for a 7:30 a.m. surgery time. Upon arrival, they guided us to our pre-op section. We were quickly visited by the anesthesiologist who, again, went over everything with us. The pulmonary care team came and spoke with us. Also, our amazing surgeon came and sat with Bracey and talked with him a bit.

He could tell Bracey was anxious, so he had the nurse give Bracey a small chewable pill that would help calm him and make him a little sleepy. This was *fabulous*! Every children's hospital should have this available. Within minutes, Bracey was completely relaxed. He was still very much alert and laughing with us but so calm and peaceful.

The nurse brought me my scrubs, and I suited up. I knew it was almost time. Pawpaw had been with us the entire time, as he creates a calming presence for Bracey. He had been playing Legos with Bracey most of this time. He and Bracey are quite inseparable and have a very special relationship. Pawpaw kissed his buddy and told him he would see Bracey soon. The grandparents came in and gave Bracey hugs and kisses and told him how excited they were for him.

Alone with Bracey, Torrey and I sat on his bed and talked about all of the fun things we were going to do after the surgery. We would get to watch the fireworks over the Mississippi River. We would get to have BBQ again. I told him we had a huge Lego kit waiting for him to build.

It was almost seven thirty. As we waited for the nurse, the three of us held hands and prayed to God.

"Lord, we thank You for the journey You have brought us on. We thank You for Your everlasting care for Bracey. We thank You for the brave boy he is. We thank You for choosing us to be his parents. We thank You for the love Bracey has for You. We thank You for the amazing team of doctors You have given us. We could not ask for a better place for Bracey to be in right now. Thank You for never giving up on us even when we questioned You. We now ask for wisdom for the doctors, nurses, and all of the medical team assigned to Bracey's care. We ask for good pain management for Bracey and for zero infections. We love You, Lord, and we will praise You in everything. Amen."

As we looked up, the nurse was standing there with tears in her eyes. She assured us God had brought us there for a reason and we were in great hands. She looked at Bracey and asked if he was ready to visit the toy tunnel. Bracey smiled and held our hands as we walked to the tunnel of toys. We finally reached the operating hallway, and we knew Torrey could not go any farther. Torrey picked up Bracey and said, "I love you, buddy. I'll be holding your hand when you wake up."

Bracey said, "I love you too, Daddy." They gave hugs and kisses, and Daddy waved goodbye as we continued to walk down the hall.

As I was choking back tears, we reached the room. We walked in and were immediately surrounded by a large group of medical professions. They all smiled at us with reassuring faces. Our doctor met us at the table. I helped Bracey up onto the table.

The nurse quickly said, "Okay, Bracey, we are going to start taking your breathing treatment just like we talked about. Are you ready?" Bracey just nodded his head yes.

I held his hands, and as he lay there breathing in the medicine, I talked about the fireworks we would see soon and the yummy BBQ ribs we would get to have. With one small tear running down his cheek, Bracey was asleep.

It happened in a matter of seconds. I was amazed at how quickly and peacefully he fell asleep. I looked over to the nurses and the doctors, and as I was crying, I said, "Thank you so much for letting me be here. Thank you for taking care of my precious son." A nurse led me out of the room and walked me down to the waiting room, where my family was waiting for me. Torrey stood up and gave me a hug. He said, "Bracey will do great. He is in amazing hands. I love you."

It was 9:30 a.m. Two hours had gone by, and a nurse came out and said the doctor was just about to start. I was shocked, but she quickly reassured me everything was fine. They had a little bit of trouble with the IVs and getting a central line in; however, everything was moving along. Bracey was doing great. His stats were excellent. She said it would still be a few more hours, but she would come out every hour and give us an update.

Our family was really good at helping us stay distracted. My sister had brought her baby girl, who really entertained us. Torrey went and got us coffee. I have always had a hard time leaving the waiting room area. I always felt like I needed to stay close by. I really don't, but it made me feel better knowing the nurses and doctors knew exactly where we were sitting and could find us at any moment.

It was 11:30 a.m. A nurse came out and said everything was going perfectly. She said it shouldn't be too much longer. She said Bracey was still doing great. He was keeping his stats up and handling the surgery beautifully.

At 1:50 p.m., six hours and twenty minutes after surgery began, the nurse came out and said Bracey was all done and the doctor would like to see us. So, Torrey, the grandparents, and I all headed to a small conference room where we waited for our doctor. We were all anxious.

I could hardly wait to see the doctor. We still didn't know if he was able to use the MAGEC rods. Mostly I just wanted to see Bracey.

Our doctor came in shortly and was carrying Bracey's 3-D model of his back. It was so cool. I hadn't seen it before. He handed it to us. As far as souvenirs go, this was a pretty cool one. The surgeon announced Bracey was a champ. He did great! He said he was able to use the MAGEC growing rods. We all cheered. We were so ecstatic that Bracey was a candidate for those rods. He said Bracey was in recovery but would be taken to the PICU shortly. We thanked and hugged him. He promised to check in with Bracey later that evening.

Within thirty minutes, a nurse was taking us to Bracey's PICU room. Typically, they only allow two at a time, but they made an exception and allowed all the grandparents to come in as well. Bracey was still very groggy when we walked in his room.

The anesthesiologist was sitting by his bed monitoring him, just as he assured us he would. Bracey was still on oxygen, with a nasal trumpet in his nose to keep his airways open.

We held Bracey's hands and began to talk to him. He nodded a few times. After about an hour, he started to open his eyes. He asked if we could remove the thing in his nose. We were so happy he was alert. Bracey stayed on oxygen, but the anesthesiologist agreed to remove the nasal trumpet.

Bracey slept the rest of the evening. He was on good medication that helped him sleep and kept him out of pain. Bracey had a fabulous night, and they decided he could move to the orthopedic floor.

July 2, 2016—Day One, Post-Op

The orthopedic floor was a much better place for us. The rooms were bigger and had space for family members to visit. Bracey was still quite sleepy, but the physical therapist came in and said she would be coming back soon and would like to get Bracey sitting up. I was not sure how he was going to sit up. He hadn't fully woken up since surgery.

About an hour later, the therapist returned and said it was time to get him to sit up. So, very slowly and cautiously, she showed us how to help Bracey sit up. He was in a back brace that had been made specifically for him. He was to wear it at all times for the next six weeks.

We watched as the therapist sat him up. He never once opened his eyes; however, he moaned a few times. The therapist helped him lie back down and said she would be in later to move him to a chair. By the end of day two, she wanted him to be taking a few steps.

July 3, 2016—Day Two, Post-Op

It was crazy how quickly they wanted Bracey on his feet. I understood the importance of it, but my baby was very hesitant. I am glad the physical therapist continued to push him even though he fought her at times and was quite annoyed.

By the second morning, the therapist helped Bracey take a short walk around the hospital floor. It was a short lap, but he did great. He did not want to do it, but he was a champ. His back was so straight. I had never seen him so straight and upright before! He looked so tall and grown-up. He still didn't say much, and he had still not eaten anything since the night before surgery. Overall, day two went better than day one. He was still very tired and very weak, but I got my first hug since surgery. I didn't want to let him go.

That evening, we finally found his favorite spot … on the couch with his wedge pillow. Once we got him situated in that spot, he was the most peaceful I had seen him since surgery. The goal since before surgery was to watch the fireworks together over the Mississippi river on July 4. I was very hopeful we would.

July 4, 2016—Day Three, Post-Op

Bracey still had very little interest in eating anything. Thankfully, we were able to supplement through his G-tube. A doctor from the orthopedic team came in early that morning to change out Bracey's bandage. It was the first time his bandage had been changed. I was anxious to see the incisions but nervous because I knew it would be uncomfortable for Bracey.

The nurse gave Bracey some medication to calm him and almost make him sleepy because they knew it would be somewhat painful. Bracey was very unhappy. It was the most pain he had been in since surgery. I sat there holding him and assuring it was almost off. As he cried on my shoulder, I just tried to reassure him it was almost over.

He began to calm down greatly. I knew the medicine had kicked in. He was practically asleep in my arms while the doctor examined his incisions. The incisions looked great. They started at the base of his neck and went down to about the top of his tail bone. He was still quite swollen, but there were no signs of infection. The doctor showed us how to clean around the incisions and how to bandage it back up. We were to apply a fresh bandage daily until the incision tape dissolved. There were no external stitches. All of his stitches were internal.

Bracey continued to take slow walks around the floor in between his naps. Bracey was still not eating but was happy drinking water. He did not like sitting up at all. We made him sit up for a few minutes and then allowed him to lie down on the couch most of the time. Unfortunately, Bracey was not up for watching the fireworks that July 4 evening. He really didn't care too much. He just couldn't keep his eyes open after a big day of walking and sitting up.

July 5, 2016

After a slow walk around the hospital floor, Bracey's doctor came in. He sat down by the couch where Bracey was lying and asked Bracey if he would like to get out of the hospital. Bracey, with a smile, nodded yes.

The doctor sat with him and explained if Bracey continued to take small walks around the floor, then he would get to go back to the big house where we were going to stay for a few more days.

Bracey asked the doctor how soon he could get his IV out. The doctor told him as long as he kept drinking, he would let the nurse take it out. Bracey agreed to keep drinking. It was also very helpful that Bracey had his G-tube. We were able to keep him hydrated and nourished through his feeding tube. The doctor gave Bracey a hug and said he would see him tomorrow in his clinic.

The nurse came and took his IV out, and Bracey perked up. He knew getting the IV out meant he was going to leave the hospital. After five days in the hospital, we were packing up and heading out! Pawpaw came and wheeled Bracey to the door. It was wonderful to be back at the big house. The house had a calming presence about it.

Brynn had been staying with my sister-in-law and her family. They drove her to Memphis that evening. It was so good to hug her. I had missed her so much. She always brought so much energy and excitement with her. She wanted to squeeze Bracey, but she understood he was very sore and she had to be gentle with him.

We spent that evening hanging out with family in the large family room where Bracey could lie on the couch. After about an hour, he was ready for some quiet time, so I took him to our room, and he quickly fell asleep.

It was great to have so much family there. We focused on Bracey while they made sure we had food in our stomachs and clean clothes to wear. Torrey's parents, Tom and Cathy, picked up Bracey's prescriptions for us and took care of Brynn, making sure she had a great time. We thank God for all of our family.

July 6, 2016

It had been six days since Bracey's surgery. He had some times of great pain and was still not eating. The doctor wanted to see him again before we left town. He changed Bracey's bandage again. Bracey had a slight fever and was very swollen, but the doctor assured us there was no infection.

Bracey had an x-ray done, and it was incredible to see the before and after x-rays. He was so straight. The doctor cleared us to go home! Bracey still struggled greatly at sitting up. Sitting was his absolute worst position.

We made a safe, comfortable bed in the car and began heading home. We drove halfway and then stopped for the evening. My parents traveled along with us as well. After we got Bracey situated in the hotel room, Torrey and I walked next door to get some food, while my parents stayed with Bracey. It was good to walk away for a few minutes and just take a break. The last six days had been exhausting, with very little sleep for both of us. That evening, Bracey slept very well. He only woke up a couple times, needing help readjusting. He was doing well, and as long as we stayed on top of his pain medication, he was pretty comfortable.

July 7, 2016

Bracey woke up that morning and, for the first time in seven days, asked for food. I was so happy! I told him anything he wanted, we would get it for him. He said he wanted his favorite breakfast restaurant, Cracker Barrel. I wasn't sure how that would work, but we tried it. Bracey could not sit on the hard wood chairs, and he wanted to stand. We ordered our drinks, and just as the waitress left, Bracey got upset and said he needed to lie down. He couldn't eat. He just wanted to go home and lie down. So, we packed up and left. It was what was best for Bracey. I hadn't really thought he would be able to handle it yet. We finally made it home about five hours later. It was so good to be home. Recovery is hard, but everything was easier to manage from home.

July 11, 2016

The next few days were tough. Bracey wanted to sleep most of the time, and when he was awake, he stood. I could not get him to sit or eat. His back was still swollen, and I am sure his doctor wished he hadn't given me his personal phone number, since I was texting him pictures of Bracey's back every day. His back was changing every day. I wanted to make sure these changes were normal at this stage in post-op surgery. His doctor was always sweet and reassuring. He promised everything was looking great.

We were shown so much love during this time. Multiple families were providing us with dinners, and Bracey received a huge Lego set he and Torrey worked on a little at a time. We were so blessed and encouraged during those long days.

By day eleven, we could tell Bracey was feeling discouraged. Torrey and I decided he needed to get out away from the house for a bit. Bracey didn't exactly want to, but we felt it would be best. It was quite hot out, and Bracey's back brace made it extra hot, so we decided to take him to the mall to walk around. We made it halfway through the mall before we knew Bracey needed to be finished. It was a lot of walking, and we were so proud of him. He didn't complain much. I think he enjoyed being out of the house for a bit. That little outing left Bracey exhausted, and he slept the rest of the day. We were determined to keep encouraging him to do something new each day.

July 17, 2016

It was seventeen days after Bracey's surgery, and he was still not eating. He remained sore and discouraged. We had tried many things, from having friends over to taking short walks on the beach, but nothing seemed to pull Bracey out of this sad funk he was in.

Torrey and I decided we all needed to get away from the house for a few days. Bracey needed a bigger distraction. So we decided to visit family in Winona Lake. We had always loved visiting the lake. Bracey would be surrounded by cousins, grandparents, and his aunt Tiph and uncle Chris.

It worked! This was the best recovery therapy we could ask for. Bracey perked up very quickly. He loved hanging out with his cousin, Reagan, and loved being at the lake. He wasn't able to get in the water that visit, but we went on a couple boat rides and watched a ski show. It was a great time and a very much needed break for our little guy.

During that visit, Bracey began to eat full meals and walk without Torrey or me helping him. He even began doing stairs. He was happy again. It was the perfect distraction and just the therapy he needed.

July 31, 2016—Eight Years Old

Bracey continued to do great. The doctor warned us that this phase in the healing process would be tough for us and Bracey because he was going to feel normal again, but he still had strict restrictions on his physical activities until his three-month post-op appointment. We joined our extended family for our annual family camping trip, and Bracey did great. We had to remind him to take it easy, and he had to continue to wear his back brace, which annoyed him, but we had a great trip. The weather was perfect. It wasn't too hot, which was a blessing since Bracey had to wear his brace anytime he was on his feet. We really felt like Bracey had made a full recovery and would be running again as soon as the doctor gave him the all clear.

August 3, 2016—Eight Years Old

It had been one month since Bracey's MAGEC rod transplant surgery. Bracey felt great. His chronic cough had greatly decreased over the last month. I was optimistic that morning as we headed to Indy for his routine checkup with his pulmonologist. I was hopeful his lung health had improved.

We walked into the doctor's office, and the nurses were amazed at how straight and tall Bracey looked. Bracey had a huge grin on his face. He walked through those doors with a confidence about him. It was obvious Bracey felt much better.

The doctor walked into our room, and she was shocked at how straight Bracey seemed. She could tell he felt better. He told her it was easier for him to breathe. She began her assessment of him, and with glassy eyes, she looked up at me and said that for the first time in over a year, she heard breath sounds in Bracey's left lung. Tears of joy streamed down my face. Thank you, Jesus! Bracey's oxygen level was 99 percent. I hadn't seen that number in years! The doctor was amazed, as was I. I had no doubt in my mind his spinal surgery was the reason his lung health had improved.

August 15, 2016—Eight Years Old

Summer disappeared as Bracey continued to amaze us. It was already the first day of school. Bracey entered third grade, and Brynn entered second. We were not sure how Bracey would do sitting most of the day, as it was still his most uncomfortable position, but he had a gracious teacher that year. She allowed Bracey to stand whenever he wanted, and he could even lie down if he needed to rest. He was still taking many breaks throughout the day, as he needed to lie down every so often. I wasn't sure if he would even make it full days. But Bracey was a trooper, and he did great. He took little breaks throughout the day, but he did awesome. All of his teachers were understanding and worked with his limitations. The start of a new school year was in the books as a success.

October 1, 2016

Exactly three months after Bracey's initial implantation of his MAGEC growing rods, we went to Memphis to visit the surgeon and have his rods lengthened for the first time. Bracey was doing amazing. I was anxious to see how the lengthening procedure was going to work. Bracey was excited to get the all clear from the doctor so he could go back to running and join in with his classmates during PE and recess.

We arrived in Memphis the day before his follow-up appointment, and we visited our favorite places again. Memphis was quickly becoming our second home. We love it down there.

Upon checking in at the doctor's office, Bracey was sent for x-rays. Soon after, the doctor came in. He sat down right by Bracey, and the two of them started talking about how school was going. Bracey told him he was ready to do PE and recess again. The doctor chuckled and agreed it was time. Bracey was so happy. The doctor looked at his back and said everything looked great. The x-rays showed the brackets had solidified to his bones and looked perfect. The rods looked great as well.

The doctor had the remote control in his hand and began to

explain to Bracey what the remote did and how it worked. He let Bracey push the buttons. The remote made a swooshing sound when operated. He showed Bracey a magnet he had in his hands and told him that magnet helped him find the two magnets in Bracey's back. He found the first magnet, and I held a mirror up so he could see it. Then the doctor said he was going to just make a small mark on his back with his purple marker and asked Bracey if that would be okay. He marked the first magnet placement, and then he found the other magnet and marked the second magnet spot. He had Bracey lie down on the bed, and with his sweet, gentle voice, he softly said he was going to begin but go very slowly.

Bracey was nervous, and I knelt down next to him and held his hands. The doctor said he could stop and give Bracey a break at any time if he needed it. It was so impressive to watch as the doctor lengthened the rods in our little guy's back. Bracey just lay there holding my hands. Within two minutes, the procedure was done. Bracey sat up.

We couldn't believe it. That was literally all there was to it! We will forever be grateful to those medical researchers who invented the MAGEC growing rods. To be able to have our child's rods lengthened every few months without surgery is priceless. No needles, no incisions, no stiches, no pain, no hospital stays, no restrictions, no risk of infections, no red lines—nothing but a loving, gentle doctor and his remote control. So, thank you to those who continue to do research on how to better the lives of our children.

Bracey was a little tender for just a few hours after the rods were lengthened. It was more of a sore muscle feeling and nothing regular Ibuprofen couldn't help manage. We gave the doctor hugs and thanked him again for being willing to try new, innovative ways to help children. I truly feel the benefits of MAGEC rods magnificently outweigh the additional cost of these rods compared to traditional rods. We told him we would see him in three months, and off we went.

Bracey's journey toward a long, healthy life was well on its way. We know Bracey will continue to have breathing issues. He will always have the severe lung disease, tracheomalacia. It's not something he will grow out of. It is a part of who he is. MAGEC growing rods have given him a fighting chance. They have allowed function in both of his lungs.

One beautiful fall evening, we took Bracey and Brynn to the park. Torrey and I sat on the bench watching as Bracey was running, climbing, swinging, and kicking the ball with friends. He wasn't standing on the sideline watching and cheering. He wasn't taking breaks because he couldn't breathe. He didn't need rest. He was in the middle, playing as hard as a little eight-year-old boy could. Torrey and I were at peace that evening as we watched Bracey's enthusiasm.

The Year 2018

I blinked, and now Bracey is almost eleven years old. The days can seem long, but the years are flying by. Bracey has had eight successful lengthening procedures of his MAGEC growing rods. He will have replacement rods put in sometime during the summer of 2019. Bracey continues to get respiratory infections; however, he has not had to be hospitalized a single time for these infections since receiving the MAGEC growing rods. Bracey will continue to have his rods lengthened every three to four months until the age of about twenty. He will have replacement rods put in every two to three years until he is finished growing, which is about the age of twenty.

Torrey started a new career in the fall of 2016, and it has flourished. In February 2018, we bought our first home. It was an exciting time for us. Our family grew in April 2018 with the surprise of our baby boy, Brevin. He truly has completed our family. Bracey and Brynn are incredible big siblings. Bracey is currently thriving in swim class and his soccer league. Brynn stays busy with drama classes and performances. She will be starting in a volleyball league in the winter of 2019. These days, I am juggling these three kids full-time. Life certainly has brought challenges, changes, laughter, and love.

Bracey is our miracle from heaven. Bracey still has challenges even to this day, but he loves his life, and he does not let his challenges stop him. He is determined to figure it out. His smile is contagious. His love for Jesus, life, family, and friends shines through his personality every day. We know just because God has a plan for our lives doesn't mean it's going to be easy. We trust He will guide us through the tough times and give us peace during those trying times and peace with the decisions we make. The best for Bracey is yet to come!

"Dear Lord, thank You for the life You have given us. I pray that I will continue to give You my worries and concerns and to ask You for guidance. You control my entire life. Sometimes my heart weighs heavy with anxiety. I pray that I always lay these anxieties before You. I thank You for holding me in Your grace. Thank You for Your constant guidance and wisdom. I pray that no matter what life brings, I will always seek You first. I love You, Lord. Amen."

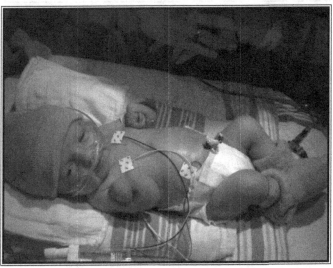

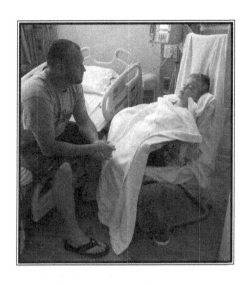

Printed in the United States
By Bookmasters